# POEMS FOR SPECIAL DAYS AND OCCASIONS

# POEMS FOR SPECIAL DAYS *and* OCCASIONS

COMPILED BY

THOMAS CURTIS CLARK, 1877-1953, comp.

*Granger Index Reprint Series*

BOOKS FOR LIBRARIES PRESS
FREEPORT, NEW YORK

Reprinted 1970 by arrangement with
Harper & Row Publishers, Inc.

INTERNATIONAL STANDARD BOOK NUMBER:
0-8369-6138-2

LIBRARY OF CONGRESS CATALOG CARD NUMBER:
76-116397

PRINTED IN THE UNITED STATES OF AMERICA

TO

HAZEL DAVIS CLARK

# NEW YEAR'S DAY

# NEW YEAR'S DAY

## PRAYER

Bless Thou this year, O Lord!
Make rich its days
With health, and work, and prayer, and praise,
And helpful ministry
To needy folk.
Speak Thy soft word
In cloudy days;
Nor let us think ourselves forgot
When common lot
Of sorrow hems us round.
Let generous impulse shame the niggard dole
That dwarfs the soul.
May no one fail his share of work
Through selfish thought;
Each day fulfill Thy holy will
In yielded lives,
And still the tumult
Of desires
Debased.
May faith, and hope, and love,
Increase.
Bless Thou this year, O Lord!

A. S. C. CLARKE.

## WHAT IS THIS COMING YEAR?

It is a door,
By which we reach new fields
Of service for our God and fellow man:
A door by which we can
Explore
Wide spheres of usefulness
Our world to bless;
And reap the sheaves God's Word of witness yields.

It is a task
Set by the Master of our souls,
A little part of our life's work below:
And so we ask
The holy wisdom, which alone controls
Our labor, teaching what and where to sow:
That the year, at its end,
May show God's glory and man's profit blend.

It is a book,
With many pages and as yet all white,
On which to write
The history of thought, and deed, and word
In this new group of days.
We pray Thee, Lord,
As Thou shalt look
Upon the book, when written o'er, may all be to Thy praise.

William Olney.

## GIFTS FOR THE NEW YEAR

Little New Year, my friend-to-be,
Come take these gifts; they are all for thee!
I give thee to laugh at many a rout
That the last little New Year wept about;
I give thee to soar where he barely crept
And to rise, alert, where he slothfully slept;
I give thee to walk with steadier tread
Past the low green grave of a pleasure dead;
I bring thee the gift of a tenderness
Which is last year's sorrow in New Year's dress;
I bring thee power that the Old Year earned
In drudging toil and in soft ease spurned;
A dusty talent from off the shelf
And a laggard will, ashamed of itself;
A broader, kindlier Charity
For the little world that I share with thee;
A Faith which the Old Year found but frail
Rising to give the New Year hail;
And brave little Hope with her dauntless smile
Ready to share the last long mile.
And best of all, lest we go astray,
You and I on the untried way,
A heavenly Guide for every day!
Little New Year, my friend-to-be,
Come take these gifts; they are all for thee!

RUBY E. WEYBURN.

## AT DAWN OF THE YEAR

Move on with a will, nor dream thou back
Though a light flashed out on the dead year's track;
Though the heart lies cold as a thing in its shroud—
There are hearts as stunned in the shifting crowd.
We move with the face toward a coming span;
We look not back where the deep seas ran!
There are lights to be struck through a darkened land.
With an onward tread and a strong right hand,
We dream again—aye, an onward dream;
We will burnish the days till they burn and gleam;
We will look not back where our light flashed out—
There are shuddering hearts we will dream about;
There are lights to be struck where hearts stand by some shroud;
We will strike if but one 'midst the shifting crowd.

GEORGE KLINGLE.

## THE OLD YEAR

What is the Old Year? 'Tis a book
On which we backward sadly look,
Not willing quite to see it close,
For leaves of violet and rose
Within its heart are thickly strewn,
Marking love's dawn and golden noon;
And turned-down pages, noting days
Dimly recalled through Memory's haze;
And tear-stained pages, too, that tell

NEW YEAR'S DAY

Of starless nights and mournful knell
Of bells tolling through trouble's air
The De Profundis of despair—
The laugh, the tear, the shine, the shade,
All 'twixt the covers gently laid;
No uncut leaves; no page unscanned;
Close it and lay it in God's hand.

CLARENCE URMY.

## A NEW LEAF

He came to my desk with quivering lip—
The lesson was done.
"Dear Teacher, I want a new leaf," he said,
"I have spoiled this one."
I took the old leaf, stained and blotted,
And gave him a new one all unspotted,
And into his sad eyes smiled,
"Do better, now, my child."

I went to the throne with a quivering soul—
The old year was done.
"Dear Father, hast Thou a new leaf for me?
I have spoiled this one."
He took the old leaf, stained and blotted,
And gave me a new one all unspotted,
And into my sad heart smiled,
"Do better, now, my child."

KATHLEEN WHEELER.

## FACING THE NEW YEAR

We pledge ourselves
To follow through the coming year
The light which God gives us:
The light of Truth, wherever it may lead;
The light of Freedom, revealing new opportunities for individual development and social service;
The light of Faith, opening new visions of the better world to be;
The light of Love, daily binding brother to brother and man to God in ever closer bonds of friendship and affection.
Guided by this light,
We shall go forward to the work of another year with steadfastness and confidence.

AUTHOR UNKNOWN.

## NEW YEARS AND OLD

Clear ringing of a bell
Beneath the midnight sky.
Some say, "It is a knell;
The Old Year has to die."
But years eternal are,
In thoughts and deeds that live.
The truth that was denied,
The sinning and the wrong,
The victories of Love
And Mercy's tender song—

NEW YEAR'S DAY

To all the coming days
Will light and shadow give.
Old Years we cannot slay,—
And would we, if we could?

No; Memory is good,
Though eyes are wet with tears
For joys that are no more;
We gather from past years
So much of wisdom's store.
If we would not blindly grope
On the road that winds ahead,
Then Experience and Hope
Must ever with us tread,
And Memory abide,
To warm the heart, and guide . . . .
Let thanks to God be said
That Old Years are not dead.

MAUD FRAZER JACKSON.

## I AM THE NEW YEAR

*I am the New Year.*

I am the one unspoiled bit of Beauty in God's Universe.

I am Romance, and Glitter, and High Resolution, and—Dreams.

My only Handicap is the dead weight of old Habits and hard-set Ways of Doing Things that I must carry over from the Past into my new ministry to your heart.

My one Fear is that some day you also will settle down to the conviction that the New is always an Illusion.

My single Hope lies in your chance Faith,

Faith that what has been proved Impossible by long experience can at last be attained;

Faith that Failure is but an Incident and not the End of the Journey;

Faith that some day, Mankind will be free from the Shackles of his own forging, Childhood will have its chance, and Love will achieve its God-like Destiny;

Faith that He who said "Behold, I make all things new" had somehow grasped the Secret for making His own Dream come true.

Faith that those who share with Him the Adventure of his Self-commitment shall find the Secret of Overflowing Life.

I am God's plan for Girding the Loins of His intrepid Co-workers in the long, but joyous march to the Goal of His Beneficent Purpose.

*I am the New Year.*

Author Unknown.

## THE LOST DAYS

As, each in turn, the Old Years rise and gird them up
  to go,
The days, which were their servitors, press round them
  sad and slow,
The happy days, the hard days, the bitter and the dear;
And they front us with reproachful eyes as they wend
  forth with the year.

## NEW YEAR'S DAY

The lost days which except for us so blessed might have
been,
Blighted by our perversity, or shadowed by our sin.
The vexing days, the moody days, the days of stress and
pain,
The shrill, perverse, unhappy days, we face them all
again.

"Come back, dear days", we cry; "we will atone for all
the wrong;
Your emptiness shall be made full, your discords turned
to song."
Only the echo answers; all vain the grieving sore.
The past is past, the dead is dead, the chance returns
no more.

But, as the sweetest hopes are born of sharpest suffering,
And midnight is the womb of day, and winter of the
spring,
So, winning blessing from despair, lost opportunity
May serve to make the fruitful soil of harvests yet to be.

For each day heavy made by us, some day may gather
wings,
Be every failure that we mourn the germ of happier
things,
And all the sadness of the past the seed of hope new-
born,
Till out of the defeated night bursts the triumphant
morn.

The old years, stern, inexorable may go their ways in vain;
The days we marred and mourn shall smile if from their perished pain
Distils a perfume, shines a gleam, to make the future way
The brighter and the easier because of yesterday.

SUSAN COOLIDGE.

## THE OLD YEAR'S PRAYER

God of the seasons, hear my parting prayer,
  Faint on the frosty air:
Let the New Year take up the work I leave,
  And finish what I weave;
Give to the troubled nations lasting peace,
  The harvest's yield increase;
Help the bereaved their sorrows to endure,
  Care for the old and poor.

Bid him give patience to all those in pain,
  And to the parched fields rain;
Protect the fledgling in its little nest,
  See that the weary rest;
And when the midnight bells from tower and town
  Send their sweet message down,
Bring faith in God, a beacon in the night
  To guide mankind aright.

MINNA IRVING.

## A NEW YEAR PRAYER

Father, I will not ask for wealth or fame,
 Though once they would have joyed my carnal sense:
I shudder not to bear a hated name,
 Wanting all wealth, myself my sole defense.
But give me, Lord, eyes to behold the truth;
 A seeing sense that knows the eternal right;
A heart with pity filled, and gentlest ruth;
 A manly faith that makes all darkness light:
Give me the power to labor for mankind;
 Make me the mouth of such as cannot speak;
Eyes let me be to groping men, and blind;
 A conscience to the base; and to the weak
Let me be hands and feet; and to the foolish, mind;
 And lead still farther on such as Thy kingdom seek.

THEODORE PARKER.

## DIARIES

The Old Year is a diary where is set
Down, page by dog-eared page, all that I knew
Of twelve months' joy, of sorrow, of regret,
A memo of the times when I was true
To trusts, to friends; what I have made of self.
Here violets are pressed . . . here is a blend
Of tears and ink . . . I'll place it on the shelf
When I have added these last words—"The End."

And now I have my New Year book to fill,
No word yet penned in it, nor any blot

Upon the clean white sheets, the pages still
Uncut, though dated day by day. Just what
They will record, God only can foretell—
And, after all, perhaps it is as well.

ETHEL ROMIG FULLER.

## FOR THE OLD YEAR

Ring the Old Year, O ring it out!
Ring the New Year and with a loud shout!
But I would hold the Old Year here
Within my hands. The things this year
Has brought to me are gay and bright—
Things of rare dreams and strange delight.
There was a hand and a soft kiss,
And one low voice that I shall miss.

There was a man who crossed my way;
And, out of them all, just one day
Will be forever mine. This year
Had many days of shadowed fear,
But that one love and that one day
Have made me want this year to stay.
Though the New Year may bring me more,
The old has added to my store
One love, one day, another friend.
Ring out! The old shall never end!

RAYMOND KRESENSKY.

## THE GOLDEN YEAR

We sleep and wake and sleep, but all things move;
The Sun flies forward to his brother Sun;
The dark Earth follows, wheeled in her ellipse;
And human things, returning on themselves,
Move onward, leading up the Golden Year.

Ah! though the times, when some new thought can bud,
Are but as poets' seasons when they flower,
Yet seas, that daily gain upon the shore,
Have ebb and flow conditioning their march,
And slow and sure comes up the Golden Year,

When wealth no more shall rest in mounded heaps,
But, smit with freer light, shall slowly melt
In many streams to fatten lower lands;
And light shall spread, and man be liker man,
Through all the seasons of the Golden Year.

Shall eagles not be eagles? wrens be wrens?
If all the world were falcons, what of that?
The wonder of the eagle were the less,
But he not less the eagle. Happy days,
Roll onward, leading up the Golden Year?

Fly, happy, happy sails, and bear the Press;
Fly, happy with the mission of the Cross;
Knit land to land, and, blowing heavenward
With silks, and fruits, and spices, clear of toll
Enrich the markets of the Golden Year.

But we grow old. Ah! when shall all men's good
Be each man's rule, and universal Peace
Lie like a shaft of light across the land,
And like a lane of beams athwart the sea,
Through all the circle of the Golden Year!

ALFRED TENNYSON.

## THE NEW YEAR

I am the New Year, and I come to you pure and unstained,
Fresh from the hand of God.
Each day, a precious pearl to you is given
That you must string upon the silver thread of Life.
Once strung can never be unthreaded but stays
An undying record of your faith and skill.
Each golden, minute link you then must weld into the chain of hours
That is no stronger than its weakest link.
Into your hands is given all the wealth and power
To make your life just what you will.
I give to you, free and unstinted, twelve glorious months
Of soothing rain and sunshine golden;
The days for work and rest, the nights for peaceful slumber.
All that I have I give with love unspoken.
All that I ask—*you keep the faith unbroken!*

J. D. TEMPLETON.

## A WAY TO A HAPPY NEW YEAR

To leave the old with a burst of song,
To recall the right and forgive the wrong;
To forget the thing that binds you fast
To the vain regrets of the year that's past;
To have the strength to let go your hold
Of the not worth while of the days grown old,
To dare go forth with a purpose true,
To the unknown task of the year that's new;
To help your brother along the road
To do his work and lift his load;
To add your gift to the world's good cheer,
Is to have and to give a Happy New Year.

ROBERT BREWSTER BEATTIE.

## THE NEW YEAR

Standing with folded wings of mystery,
The New Year waits to greet us—you and me.

Her arms are full of gifts, her feet are shod
All fitly for rough roads or velvet sod;
Her eyes are steady with belief in God.

Her voice falls sweetly as a vesper bell
Where trust and hope all lesser notes dispel;
Scarce knowing why, we feel that all is well.

She smiles a little ere she turns away,
Breathing a promise for each coming day;
And we—we pause a little while to pray.

AUTHOR UNKNOWN.

# LINCOLN'S BIRTHDAY

# LINCOLN'S BIRTHDAY

## MASTER, MAKE US ONE!

Great brother to the lofty and the low,
Our tears, our tears give tribute! A dark throng,
With fetters of hereditary wrong
Chained, serf-like, in the choking dust of woe,
Lifts up its arms to you, lifts up its cries!
Oh, you, who knew all anguish, in whose eyes,
Pity, with tear-stained face,
Kept her long vigil o'er the severed lands
For friend and foe, for race and race;
You, to whom all were brothers, by the strands
Of spirit, of divinity,
Bound not to color, church, or sod,
Only to man, only to God;
You, to whom all beneath the sun
Moved to one hope, one destiny—
Lover of liberty, oh, make us free!
Lover of union, Master, make us one!

HERMANN HAGEDORN.

*From* Lincoln: An Ode

## *From* LINCOLN, THE MAN OF THE PEOPLE

The color of the ground was in him, the red earth,
The smack and tang of elemental things:
The rectitude and patience of the cliff,

The good-will of the rain that loves all leaves,
The friendly welcome of the wayside well,
The courage of the bird that dares the sea,
The gladness of the wind that shakes the corn,
The pity of the snow that hides all scars,
The secrecy of streams that make their way
Under the mountain to the rifted rock,
The tolerance and equity of light
That gives as freely to the shrinking flower
As to the great oak flaring to the wind—
To the grave's low hill as to the Matterhorn
That shoulders out the sky.

. . . . . . . . .

So came the Captain with the mighty heart;
And when the judgment thunders split the house,
Wrenching the rafters from their ancient rest,
He held the ridgepole up, and spiked again
The rafters of the Home. He held his place—
Held the long purpose like a growing tree—
Held on through blame and faltered not at praise—
Towering in calm rough-hewn sublimity.
And when he fell in whirlwind, he went down
As when a lordly cedar, green with boughs,
Goes down with a great shout upon the hills,
And leaves a lonesome place against the sky.

EDWIN MARKHAM.

## LINCOLN

He labored in a lonely field,
  Yet sometimes I have thought
He glimpsed a Figure distant there,

LINCOLN'S BIRTHDAY

As patiently he wrought
Through aching stillnesses, wherein
He toiled, and murmured not.

How often, in the anguished hours
He felt and understood
The lonely Man who watched afar
So sorrowful, so good;
The silent Friend, whose presence there
Gave solace to his mood.

Surely he felt Him near, when men
Forsook and fled the place!
When all he knew of comforting
Was in that changeless grace;
Surely, in his Gethsemane
He must have seen His face!

LAURA SIMMONS.

## THE GREAT AMERICAN

Not out of the East but the West
A Star and a Savior arose;
A light to an eager quest,
A spirit of grace possessed,
Of faith 'mid increasing woes,
Of wisdom manifest,
And, forth from the variant past
Of thraldom's darkness, at last
God's measureless love for man
Wrought through heredity's dower

The great American,
Whose soul was the perfect flower
Of patriot planting in soil
Kept moist by blood and tears,
And fertile by faithful toil
Throughout unnumbered years.

LYMAN WHITNEY ALLEN.

*From* The Star of Sangamon.

## HE IS NOT DEAD

He is not dead. France knows he is not dead;
He stirs strong hearts in Spain and Germany,
In far Siberian mines his words are said;
He calls poor serfs about him in the night,
And whispers of a power that laughs at kings,
And of a force that breaks the strongest chain;
Old tyranny feels his might
Tearing away its deepest fastenings,
And jeweled scepters threaten him in vain.

Years pass away, but freedom does not pass,
Thrones crumble, but man's birthright crumbles not,
And, like the wind across the prairie grass,
A whole world's aspirations fan this spot
With ceaseless panting after liberty,
One breath of which would make dark Russia fair,
And blow sweet summer through the exile's cave,
And set the exile free;
For which I pray, here in the open air
Of Freedom's morning-tide, by Lincoln's grave.

MAURICE THOMPSON.

*From* Lincoln's Grave.

## LINCOLN

Chained by stern duty to the rock of State,
His spirit armed in mail of rugged mirth,
Ever above, though ever near to earth,
Yet felt his heart the cruel tongues that sate
Base appetites, and foul with slander, wait
Till the keen lightnings bring the awful hour
When wounds and suffering shall give them power.
Most was he like to Luther, gay and great,
Solemn and mirthful, strong of heart and limb.
Tender and simple too; he was so near
To all things human that he cast out fear,
And, ever simpler, like a little child,
Lived in unconscious nearness unto Him
Who always on earth's little ones hath smiled.

S. Weir Mitchell.

## THE CENOTAPH OF LINCOLN

And so they buried Lincoln! Strange and vain!
Has any creature thought of Lincoln hid
In any vault, 'neath any coffin lid,
In all the years since that wild spring of pain?
'Tis false—he never in the grave hath lain.
You could not bury him although you slid
Upon his clay the Cheops pyramid
Or heaped it with the Rocky Mountain chain.
They slew themselves; they but set Lincoln free.
In all the earth his great heart beats as strong,

Shall beat while pulses throb to chivalry
And burn with hate of tyranny and wrong.
Whoever will may find him anywhere
Save in the tomb—not there, he is not there.

JAMES T. MACKAY.

## ABRAHAM LINCOLN

This man whose homely face you look upon
Was one of Nature's masterful great men,
Born with strong arms that unfought victories won.
Direct of speech, and cunning with the pen,
Chosen for large designs, he had the art
Of winning with his humor, and he went
Straight to his mark, which was the human heart.
Wise, too, for what he could not break, he bent;
Upon his back, a more than Atlas load,
The burden of the Commonwealth was laid;
He stooped and rose up with it, though the road
Shot suddenly downwards, not a whit dismayed.
Hold, warriors, councilors, kings! All now give place
To this dead Benefactor of the Race.

RICHARD HENRY STODDARD.

## LINCOLN AT GETTYSBURG

The whole world came to hear him speak that day
And all the ages sent their scribes to see
And hear what word the new land had to say

Of God and man and truth and liberty.
Homer was there and Socrates and Paul,
Shakespeare and Luther, Pitt, Cavour, and Bright,
With Washington—staunch friends of freedom all;
Nor did he fail: he lifted there a light
For all the earth to see, from fires of truth
That surged within his breast. Yet that crude throng
Of men knew not that through this man uncouth
God spake as through old prophets, stern and strong.
They turned away, these men, but angels bent
From heaven to hear those flaming words, God-sent.

THOMAS CURTIS CLARK.

## LINCOLN'S GETTYSBURG ADDRESS
(November 19, 1863)

Fourscore and seven years ago our fathers brought forth upon this continent a new nation,
Conceived in liberty, and dedicated to the proposition that all men are created equal.

Now we are engaged in a great civil war, testing whether that nation, or any nation, so conceived and so dedicated, can long endure.
We are met on a great battlefield of that war.
We have come to dedicate a portion of that field as a final resting place for those who here gave their lives that that nation might live.
It is altogether fitting and proper that we should do this.

But in a larger sense we cannot dedicate, we cannot consecrate, we cannot hallow this ground.
The brave men, living and dead, who struggled here, have consecrated it far above our poor power to add or detract.
The world will little note nor long remember what we say here,
But it can never forget what they did here.

It is for us, the living, rather, to be dedicated here to the unfinished work which they who fought here have thus far so nobly advanced.
It is rather for us to be here dedicated to the great task remaining before us;
That from these honored dead we take increased devotion to that cause for which they gave the last full measure of devotion;
That we here highly resolve that these dead shall not have died in vain;
That this nation, under God, shall have a new birth of freedom;
And that government of the people, by the people, and for the people,
Shall not perish from the earth.

## THE MARTYR CHIEF

Nature, they say, doth dote,
And cannot make a man
Save on some worn-out plan,
Repeating as by rote:

## LINCOLN'S BIRTHDAY

For him her Old-World moulds aside she threw,
And, choosing sweet clay from the breast
Of the unexhausted West,
With stuff untainted shaped a hero new,
Wise, steadfast in the strength of God, and true.

. . . . . . . .

His was no lonely mountain-peak of mind,
Thrusting to thin air o'er our cloudy bars,
A seamark now, now lost in vapors blind,
Broad prairie rather, genial, level-lined,
Fruitful and friendly for all human kind.

. . . . . . . .

Great captains, with their guns and drums,
Disturb our judgment for the hour,
But at last silence comes:
These are all gone, and, standing like a tower,
Our children shall behold his fame,
The kindly-earnest, brave, foreseeing man,
Sagacious, patient, dreading praise, not blame,
New birth of our new soil, the first American.

JAMES RUSSELL LOWELL.

## LINCOLN

A blend of mirth and sadness
Of smiles and tears,
A quaint knight errant
Of the pioneers.
A homely hero
Of star and sod,
A peasant prince,
A masterpiece of God.

WALTER MALONE.

# WASHINGTON'S BIRTHDAY

# WASHINGTON'S BIRTHDAY

## WASHINGTON AND LINCOLN

Two stars alone of primal magnitude,
Twin beacons in our firmament of fame,
Shine for all men with benison the same:
On day's loud labor by the night renewed,
On templed silences where none intrude,
On leaders followed by the street's acclaim,
The solitary student by his flame,
The watcher in the battle's interlude.
All ways and works of men they shine upon;
And now and then beneath their golden light
A sudden meteor reddens and is gone;
And now and then a star grows strangely bright,
Drawing all eyes, then dwindles in the night;
And the eternal sentinels shine on.

WENDELL PHILLIPS STAFFORD.

## ODE FOR WASHINGTON'S BIRTHDAY

Welcome to the day returning,
  Dearer still as ages flow,
While the torch of Faith is burning,
  Long as Freedom's altars glow!
See the hero whom it gave us
  Slumbering on a mother's breast;

For the arm he stretched to save us,
Be its morn forever blest!

. . . .

Vain is Empire's mad temptation!
Not for him an earthly crown!
He whose sword hath freed a nation
Strikes the offered scepter down.
See the throneless Conqueror seated,
Ruler by a people's choice;
See the Patriot's task completed;
Hear the Father's dying voice!

"By the name that you inherit,
By the sufferings you recall,
Cherish the fraternal spirit;
Love your country first of all!
Listen not to idle questions
If its bands may be untied;
Doubt the patriot whose suggestions
Strive a nation to divide!"

Father! We, whose ears have tingled
With the discord-notes of shame—
We, whose sires their blood have mingled
In the battle's thunder-flame—
Gathering, while this holy morning
Lights the land from sea to sea,
Hear thy counsel, heed thy warning;
Trust us, while we honor thee!

OLIVER WENDELL HOLMES.

## INSCRIPTION AT MT. VERNON

Washington, the brave, the wise, the good,
Supreme in war, in council, and in peace.
Valiant without ambition, discreet without fear, confident without assumption.
In disaster calm, in success moderate; in all, himself.
The hero, the patriot, the Christian.
The father of nations, the friend of mankind,
Who, when he had won all, renounced all, and sought in the bosom of his family and of nature, retirement, and in the hope of religion, immortality.

## WASHINGTON

Long are the years since he fell asleep
Where the Potomac flows gently by,
There where Mt. Vernon's green stretches sweep
Under the blue Virginia sky.
Warrior and statesman and patriot true,
Well had he wielded both sword and pen.
Truly, they said as they laid him to rest,
"First in the hearts of his countrymen."

Long are the years—and the land he loved
Stands among nations, grown strong and great;
True to his vision of long ago,
Proud of the hand that so shaped her fate.

Time but adds splendor to fame so fair,
  Years but test greatness—and now as then
Sleeps he in peace on Mt. Vernon's hill,
  "First in the hearts of his countrymen."

B. Y. Williams.

## WASHINGTON

Soldier and statesman, rarest unison;
High-poised example of great duties done
Simply as breathing, a world's honors worn
As life's indifferent gifts to all men born;
Dumb for himself, unless it were to God,
But for his barefoot soldier eloquent,
Tramping the snow to coral where they trod,
Held by his awe in hollow-eyed content;
Modest, yet firm as Nature's self; unblamed
Save by the men his nobler temper shamed;
Not honored then or now because he wooed
The popular voice, but that he still withstood;
Broad-minded, higher-souled, there is but one
Who was all this and ours and all men's—Washington.

James Russell Lowell.

## WASHINGTON

O noble brow, so wise in thought!
O heart so true! O soul unbought!
O eye so keen to pierce the night,
And guide the ship of state aright!

## WASHINGTON'S BIRTHDAY

O life so simple, grand and free;
The humblest still may turn to thee.
O king uncrowned! O prince of men!
When shall we see thy like again?

MARY WINGATE.

## THE GREAT VIRGINIAN

Never to see a nation born, hath been given to mortal man,
Unless to those who on that summer morn
Gazed silent when the great Virginian
Unsheathed the sword whose fatal flash
Shot union through the incoherent clash
Of our loose atoms, crystallizing them
Around a single will's unpliant stem,
And making purpose of emotions rash.
Out of that scabbard sprang as from its womb,
Nebulous at first, but hardening to a star,
Through mutual share of sunburst and of gloom,
The common faith that makes us what we are.

JAMES RUSSELL LOWELL.

# LENT AND EASTER

# LENT AND EASTER

## REALITY

Not from two who supped with You
At an inn as twilight fell
Do I know that Joseph's tomb
Was an empty shell.
Not from Peter or from John
Or from Mary or from Paul
Did I learn how life can change
At Your call.

Not on the Damascus road
Or in any far off place
Did my spirit see the dawn
Of Your face.
Those who lived in Galilee
Knew their Lord and held Him dear—
But my Lord has come to me
Now and here.

AMELIA JOSEPHINE BURR.

## MARY

Beside the empty sepulchre she lingered
With tear-dimmed eyes, and heart with sorrow worn,
Nor heeded One whose Presence in that garden
A radiance shed, surpassing that of morn!

He stood beside her (tho' her eyes were holden)
  Then spoke her name, in accents low and sweet;
And at that long-loved voice she turned in rapture,
  Beheld her Lord, and worshipped at His Feet!

So speak to us, dear Lord, amid earth's shadows,
  When doubts and fears oppress the human heart;
And at Thy Voice shall break the light of morning,
  Revealing Thee, all-glorious as Thou art!

W. B.

## *From* GETHSEMANE

All those who journey, soon or late,
Must pass within the garden's gate;
Must kneel alone in darkness there,
And battle with some fierce despair.
God pity those who cannot say:
"Not mine but thine"; who only pray:
"Let this cup pass," and cannot see
The purpose in Gethsemane.

Ella Wheeler Wilcox.

## EASTER

With song and sun-burst comes the Easter morn:
Yet was there sunset ere the sun arose;
Under the sod, the rain-drift and the snows,
The nurturing of life, wherefrom was born
The blossom on the breast of beauty worn.
Each way of glory through some garden goes
Where midnight yet a deeper midnight knows,

Against the halo, cross and scourge and thorn.
Will it be always so? the Easter still
Always the answer to what seemeth ill?
Or shall we some day know that all is good
If but the all, at last, be understood?
This the consummate Easter that shall be
In the full sun-burst of Eternity!

ROBERT WHITAKER.

## THE UNBELIEVABLE

Impossible, you say, that man survives
The grave—that there are other lives?
More strange, O friend, that we should ever rise
Out of the dark to walk below these skies
Once having risen into life and light,
We need not wonder at our deathless flight.

Life is the unbelievable; but now
That this Incredible has taught us how,
We can believe the all-imagining Power
That breathed the Cosmos forth as a golden flower,
Had potence in his breath
To plan us new surprises beyond death—
New spaces and new goals
For the adventure of ascending souls.

Be brave, O heart, be brave:
It is not strange that man survives the grave:
'Twould be a stranger thing were he destroyed
Than that he ever vaulted from the void.

EDWIN MARKHAM.

## "TELL THE DISCIPLES"

Into the tomb they took Him, sad of heart,
And rolled the stone, then turned aside apart
  To mourn each one the unfulfilled fair dream
To which their dead hopes could no life impart.

Back to the tomb they went at break of day.
The stone that sealed the tomb was rolled away!
  Frightened they looked, and heard the words of joy,
"Fear not: for He is risen. Go your way,

"Tell the disciples." From the tomb they came,
Renewed in hope; with eyes alight, they bare
  Christ risen in their hearts, alive, not dead—
And, lo, He has been with them everywhere!

AUTHOR UNKNOWN.

## CHRIST ON THE CROSS

They raised Him on the road and pierced Him through.
He cried, "Forgive them, Father: what they do
  They know not." Yea, it smote Him to the heart
To know this monstrous wrong of them was true.

Then to the thief who prayed "Remember me,"
He said, "This day in Paradise thou'lt be
  With me"; and to His mother, bathed in tears,
"Behold thy son"; to John, "Thy mother see."

The soldiers heard Him when His pain was worst,
"God, why hast thou forsaken me?" They cursed,

Half-pitying Him at sight of His drawn face,
And turning toward Him then. He said, "I thirst."

They brought Him vinegar to ease the end.
"Into Thy hands, my Father, I commend
My spirit."—"It is finished," last He said.—
O Christ, this hearing, we our ways would mend!

We who are brethren of the howling throng
That cried for murder, bitterly and long,
And cheered the soldiers cursing at the tree,
Would mend our ways, our still Christ-slaying wrong!

AUTHOR UNKNOWN.

## THE PRIESTS AND SOLDIERS

While there He hung, the scoffing Levites cried,
"Heal now thyself: come down, the cross beside!"
Exulting in their power none dared dispute,
By which this upstart scribe they crucified.

They held the power in Zion, and they thought
They were securer for the death-stroke brought
Upon the meek head mockingly thorn-crowned,
To signify the Kingdom come to naught.

How could they know, who forced the crimson shower
From His pierced palms and feet, their own Dark Hour
Gloomed at them from the clouds, and at each blow
That sank the nails, strength ebbed from out their power?

They thought, whom Caesar sent, the sun on high
Was kindled for their Rome to rule men by,
   And chaffed the still Man hanging on the cross,
Mocked Him from hearts meshed in fatuity,

Scoffed at Him, crying, "Rome shall stand for aye,
O Fool!"—elate that they could take and slay,
   By strength, each little king that dared to raise
His rebel banner in Rome's conquering way.

The true fools they! Their boasting mouths are long
Mixed with the dust, and Him they blithely hung
   And speared, they slew too late to save their world:
Dying, He took the world from them, the strong.

AUTHOR UNKNOWN.

## I WOULD GO BACK

I would go back and sit beside His feet,
   Far from the swaying argument of men,
So listening humbly to the cadence sweet
   Of that dear Voice would know the truth as then.

How simple, just to lean in that quiet place,
   Remote from controversy and vexed strife,
And hear, rapt, gazing upward on His Face,
   Fall from His Lips the jeweled words of Life.

Not where men's errors, subtly wove, disclose
   A glittering Serpent that uprears and stings
Till hearts are broke—but here the spirit grows
   'Mid mountain peace, and brooding sense of wings.

What is the Faith that I shall call for mine
  Creed of my fathers, reverenced in my heart?
Nay, far more high, more sacred more Divine—
  That boundless Love Christ teacheth far apart.

MARY M. CURCHOD.

## GETHSEMANE

Breathes there a man who claimeth not
  One lonely spot,
    His own Gethsemane,
Whither with his inmost pain
He fain
  Would weary plod,
Find the surcease that is known
In wind a-moan
  And sobbing sea,
Cry his sorrow hid of men,
And then—
  Touch hands with God.

EDMUND LEAMY.

## HOST AND GUEST

  I may not claim
Entrance to Thy high feast, so sin-marred I;
  And yet, for all my shame,
Some scattered crumbs I crave before I die.
"Lo! at Thy door I knock, and I will be
In Thine own house Thy guest, and sup with Thee."

How shall I spread
A table Thou canst condescend to share?
How shall my coarse-made bread
And tasteless wine for Thee prove fitting fare?
"Lo! My own flesh and blood, to salve Thy need,
I bring—and these are meat and drink indeed."

No robe is mine
Wherein I may, when once is set the board,
Close at Thy side recline,
With Thy fair splendor matched in due accord.
"Lo! I bestow on Thee, for ample dress
The glorious garment of My righteousness."

HENRY W. CLARK.

## FOR US

If we have not learned that God's in man,
And man in God again,
That to love thy God is to love thy brother,
And to serve thy Lord is to serve each other—
Then Christ was born in vain!

If we have not learned that one man's life
In all men lives again;
That each man's battle, fought alone,
Is won or lost for everyone—
Then Christ hath lived in vain!

If we have not learned that death's no break
  In life's unceasing chain,
That the work in one life well begun
In others is finished, by others is done—
  Then Christ hath died in vain!

If we have not learned of immortal life,
  And a future free from pain,
The Kingdom of God in the heart of man,
And the living world on heaven's plan—
  Then Christ arose in vain!

CHARLOTTE PERKINS GILMAN.

## PALM SUNDAY HYMN

Looking back across the years, O Christ, we see Thee go
Midst hosannas of the throngs passing to and fro,
Midst the adoration cries ringing on Thy way—
Voices of the wavering ones lifted for a day.

We hosannas echo on, O Christ, and lift to Thee
Songs of adoration too, and bend adoring knee,
But, though faltering and weak, may we not forget
Like the throngs of long ago, the Heart that loveth yet.

Help us follow all the way, O Christ, nor turn aside.
Midst Thy shadows, or Thy light, there would we abide,
Though the world hath scarred Thy name, mark it on
  our breast—
Sweetest name in all the world that ever Love confessed.

GEORGE KLINGLE.

## BUTTERFLY

I am the worm
  that dared to dream
    a dream beyond belief;

I am the worm
  that made me a bed
    and lay in a silken sheaf.

I dreamed it deep
  and I dreamed it true
    that a worm might rise and fly—

That I might awake
  a flying flower
    in a blowing heaven of sky.

MARY WHITE SLATER.

## I SHALL LIVE ON

I am in love with life,
  And it must be
That Life shall be in
  Love with me;
I shall live on!
Across what unknown sea
  Or shore I go?
I do not know;
But that I shall live on,
  I know, I know!

### LENT AND EASTER

A Voice, more deep than death,
  Says it is so;
I am in love with life,
  And it must be
That Life shall be in
  Love with me.

RALPH S. CUSHMAN.

## DEATH

No learned discussion
On the soul's immortality;
No treatment of original sin;
No theories concerning
Self and not-self;
No treatise on the atonement—
Do we hear
When we stand confounded
By Death.

Jesus understands and says:
"Let not your heart be troubled;
The child has gone
To our Father."
And we are comforted.

ETNA DOOP-SMITH.

## YOUTH AND DEATH

Death is but life's escape: a rung
On which life climbs from where it clung
To a new height of youth. Forever
Death clogs our feet in vain endeavor
To hold us—trying still to keep
Life fast in habit, ease, or sleep,
In sluggard blood and ageing brain. . . .
Forever life breaks free again,
Outwitting death by death. We perish
To wake us from the graves we cherish.
We lose—that youth may gain—our breath;
And God remains alive by death.

E. MERRILL ROOT.

## THE REFUGEE

They told me Death had lost its sting, and yet
Their white lips trembled. Though their words were free,
Their tones fell, muffled in mortality.
And I—who thought I never could forget
The voice beneath the leaves of Olivet,
The futile tomb, the tryst in Galilee—
Felt the old fear, with man, the refugee,
And over life and love, Death's ancient threat.

It loomed, a wall across the winding years—
A ponderous breaker roaring through blurred ears—
An aching distance where beloved souls go

With backward looks through long, cold leagues of
night.
Then, round a bend, I came on Death, and lo!
A flimsy curtain blowing into light!

HELEN MOLYNEAUX SALISBURY.

## IF EASTER BE NOT TRUE

If Easter be not true,
Then all the lilies low must lie;
The Flanders poppies fade and die;
The spring must lose her fairest bloom
For Christ were still within the tomb—
If Easter be not true.

If Easter be not true,
Then faith must mount on broken wing;
Then hope no more immortal spring;
Then hope must lose her mighty urge;
Life prove a phantom, death a dirge—
If Easter be not true.

If Easter be not true,
'Twere foolishness the cross to bear;
He died in vain who suffered there;
What matter though we laugh or cry,
Be good or evil, live or die,
If Easter be not true?

If Easter be not true—
But it is true, and Christ is risen!
And mortal spirit from its prison

Of sin and death with Him may rise!
Worthwhile the struggle, sure the prize,
Since Easter, aye, is true!

HENRY H. BARSTOW.

## AN EASTER PRAYER

Lord, now that spring is in the world,
And every tulip is a cup
Filled with the wine of Thy great love,
Lift thou me up.

Raise Thou my heart as flowers arise
To greet the glory of Thy day,
With soul as clean as lilies are,
And white as they.

Let me not fear the darkness now,
Since Life and Light break through Thy tomb;
Teach me that doubts no more oppress,
No more consume.

Show me that Thou art April, Lord,
And Thou the flowers and the grass;
Then, when awake the soft spring winds,
I'll hear Thee pass!

CHARLES HANSON TOWNE.

## WHAT DOES EASTER MEAN TO YOU?

What does Easter mean to you?
Stately church with cushioned pew,
Where, Lenten season gone at last
And days of self-denial past,
Richly-clad, devoted throngs
Of worshippers unite in songs
Of praise in lily-scented air?
Is this what makes your Easter fair?

Does it mean the end of winter's reign,
Bright skies and welcome warmth again,
Singing of birds, budding of trees,
Sweet spring odors on the breeze
From daffodil and crocus bed
And balsam branches overhead?
Sad is the world and cold and gray,
If this is all of Easter Day.

But if this blessed season brings
A firmer faith in holy things;
Assurance of a living Lord;
A strengthening of the tender chord
Of love that binds us to the life to come
Where loved ones 'wait us in the heavenly home,
No pain or loss can e'er efface the bliss,
Dear friend, of Easter when it means all this.

MAY RICKER CONRAD.

## THE WOUNDED CHRIST-HEART

Anew He is wounded! The barbs of His wounding
Are hurled by His children, those marked with His name,
Who carry His banners, who ring forth hosannas—
These robe Him with shame.

Anew He is wounded. The Temple He builded,
The fabric He reared from the stream of His blood,
Is shivered with echoes that score Him, that shame Him—
Who built with His blood.

The Soul-of-the-world is aghast at its moorings—
The rock of its faith that standeth secure—
It is racked by the breakers of sound that beat over;
Keen voices that follow Time's lure.

Oh the Voices! These Voices, all barbèd that bruise Him;
His own children's voices, once pledged and apart,
That shame Him—the Christ of the World—soul immortal—
They wound the Christ-heart.

GEORGE KLINGLE.

## CALVARY AND EASTER

A song of sunshine through the rain,
Of spring across the snow;
A balm to heal the hurts of pain,
A peace surpassing woe.

## LENT AND EASTER

Lift up your heads, ye sorrowing ones,
  And be ye glad of heart,
For Calvary and Easter Day
  Were just three days apart!

With shudder of despair and loss
  The world's deep heart is wrung,
As, lifted high upon His cross,
  The Lord of Glory hung—
When rocks were rent, and ghostly forms
  Stole forth in street and mart;
But Calvary and Easter Day,
Earth's blackest day, and whitest day,
  Were just three days apart.

AUTHOR UNKNOWN.

## EASTER CAROL

O Earth! throughout thy borders
  Re-don thy fairest dress;
And everywhere, O Nature!
  Throb with new happiness;
Once more to new creation
  Awake, and death gainsay,
For death is swallowed up of life,
  And Christ is risen today!

Let peals of jubilation
  Ring out in all the lands;
With hearts of deep elation
  Let sea with sea clasp hands;

I stumble on as in the night,
And do not see the shafts of dawn.

But oh, the joy of faring, Lord,
On ways Thy sandalled feet have trod,
Where all Thy kindly words and deeds
Illume the path that leads to God.

Where Thou hast walked is safe for me
There beauty and all truth are found;
My heart upsprings at every step
I take upon his hallowed ground!

VERNA LOVEDAY HARDEN.

## RESURRECTION

Who knows the quiet road beyond the silence? . . .
Why! no one that has e'er returned to tell;
But He that holds the measure-rod of ages
Knows every step of it—and it is well.
He measured it to fit the souls He'd fashioned;
He made it beautiful, wonderful as birth,
And bordered it with mercy and compassion,
And lit it with the love that crowns the earth.
He paved it with His gracious care, remembering
The weary journey for the stumbling feet,
And set it in a peace that passeth knowledge,
Where He Himself awaits His own to greet.

BLODWEN DAVIES.

## GOOD FRIDAY

We carve His Cross into an amulet,
The red blood which He shed upon the hill
We make a rite of worship, and forget
The red religion of courageous will.

Hugh O. Isbell.

## THE STONE

"Christ is risen, Christ is risen!",
The glad voices glibly say,
Yet He lies within the prison
Of our stolid hearts today.

No angel rolls away the stone
Of cowardice and greed.
It is our strength and ours alone
Can answer for that need.

Grant us strength in straining, lifting,
He on His side, we on ours,
Till at length, the boulder shifting,
Christ comes forth among the flowers.

Kenneth W. Porter.

# MOTHER'S DAY

# MOTHER'S DAY

## THE GREATEST BATTLE THAT EVER WAS FOUGHT

The greatest battle that ever was fought—
  Shall I tell you where and when?
On the maps of the world you will find it not:
  It was fought by the Mothers of Men.

Not with cannon or battle shot,
  With sword or nobler pen;
Not with eloquent word or thought
  From the wonderful minds of men;

But deep in a walled up woman's heart;
  A woman that would not yield;
But bravely and patiently bore her part;
  Lo! there is that battlefield.

No marshalling troops, no bivouac song,
  No banner to gleam and wave;
But Oh these battles they last so long—
  From babyhood to the grave!

But faithful still as a bridge of stars
  She fights in her walled up town;
Fights on, and on, in the endless wars;
  Then silent, unseen goes down!

Ho! ye with banners and battle shot,
With soldiers to shout and praise,
I tell you the kingliest victories fought
Are fought in these silent ways.

JOAQUIN MILLER.

## FAITH OF OUR MOTHERS

Faith of our mothers, living faith,
In cradle song and bedtime prayer,
In nursery love and fireside lore,
Thy presence still pervades the air;
Faith of our mothers, living faith,
We will be true to thee till death.

Faith of our mothers, guiding faith,
For youthful longing, youthful doubt,
How blurred our vision, blind our way,
Thy providential care without;
Faith of our mothers, guiding faith,
We will be true to thee till death.

Faith of our mothers, Christian faith,
In truth beyond our man-made creeds,
Still save the home and save the church,
And breathe thy spirit through our deeds;
Faith of our mothers, Christian faith,
We will be true to thee till death.

AUTHOR UNKNOWN.

## MOTHER LOVE

I bent my ears to a lily's cup,
And thought that it spoke to me
By the stainless white of its petals light,
Of a Mother's purity.

To the heart of a red, red rose I crushed
And it seemed that within my eyes
There was shadowed the gleam of the crimson stream
Of a Mother's sacrifice.

I considered the sun and the moon and the stars,
The winds, and the tides of the sea,
And found in the span of their beautiful plan
All a Mother's constancy.

Then I lifted my eyes to a hilltop lone,
Where Love hung high on a tree.
And lo, it was there I could best compare
My Mother's love for me!

Janie Alford.

## MOTHER—A PORTRAIT

Her hands have much
Of Christ-like touch.

Her smile on one
Is benison.

Her silver hair,
A halo rare.

Her step, a sound
On Holy ground.

Her dear face lined,
But kind—kind.

Of women, best
And loveliest.

ETHEL ROMIG FULLER.

## WONDROUS MOTHERHOOD

Thank God! for that lovely spirit
That makes motherhood akin.
They have known the way of travail.
They have known the pangs of pain.
They have compassed hope and sorrow.
They have had both tears and joy.
That is why a glowing radiance
Shines in all they say and do.
That is why they are the blessed,
Why we hail them far and wide
Dearest of all God's creations,
Great and wondrous motherhood.

AUTHOR UNKNOWN.

## "HAPPY HE WITH SUCH A MOTHER"

I loved her: one
Not learned, save in gracious household ways,
Nor perfect, nay, but full of tender wants;
No angel, but a dearer being, all dipt
In angel instincts, breathing Paradise,
Interpreter between the gods and men,
Who looked all native to her place and yet
On tiptoe seemed to touch upon a sphere
Too gross to tread, and all male minds perforce
Swayed to her from their orbits as they moved
And girdled her with music. Happy he
With such a mother; faith in womenkind
Beats with his blood, and trusts in all things high
Come easy to him, and though he trip and fall,
He shall not blind his soul with clay.

ALFRED TENNYSON.

## LOVE'S MAGIC

Were I possessed of an alchemy rare,
  Do you know, Mother of Mine, what I'd do?
I'd sift out the gold from the rays of the sun
  And bring it, a gift, for you.

Were I a weaver with magical skill,
  Do you know, Mother of Mine, what I'd do?
I'd spin silv'ry threads from the beams of the moon
  And fashion a gown for you.

Were I a magician with power supreme,
Do you know, Mother of Mine, what I'd do?
I'd change drops of rain and the dew into pearls
And string them, a necklace, for you.

But I'm just a poor singer, without skill or power.
This only, dear mother, can I do,
I make these vain dreams into melodies sweet
And sing them, in love, to you.

CLARA CARSON LELAND.

## THE MOTHER OF THE HOUSE

Strength and dignity are her clothing;
And she laugheth at the time to come.
She openeth her mouth to wisdom;
And the law of kindness is in her tongue.
She looketh well to the ways of her household,
And eateth not the bread of idleness;
Her children rise up and call her blessed,
Her husband, also, and he praiseth her, saying:
"Many daughters have done virtuously,
But thou excelleth them all."

PROVERBS 31:25-29.

## DEAR OLD MOTHERS

I love old mothers—mothers with white hair
And kindly eyes, and lips grown soft and sweet
With murmured blessings over sleeping babes.
There is something in their quiet grace

That speaks the calm of Sabbath afternoons;
A knowledge in their deep, unfaltering eyes
That far outreaches all philosophy.

Time, with caressing touch about them weaves
The silver-threaded fairy-shawl of age,
While all the echoes of forgotten songs
Seem joined to lend sweetness to their speech.

Old mothers! as they pass with slow-timed step,
Their trembling hands cling gently to youth's strength.
Sweet mothers!—as they pass, one sees again
Old garden-walks, old roses, and old loves.

CHARLES S. ROSS.

## OUR MOTHERS

O magical word, may it never die from the lips that love to speak it,
Nor melt away from the trusting hearts that even would break to keep it.
Was there ever a name that lived like thine! Will there ever be another?
The angels have reared in heaven a shrine to the holy name of Mother.

AUTHOR UNKNOWN.

## MOTHER'S LOVE

Her love is like an island
In life's ocean, vast and wide,
A peaceful, quiet shelter
From the wind, and rain, and tide.

'Tis bound on the north by Hope,
By Patience on the west,
By tender Counsel on the south,
And on the east by Rest.

Above it like a beacon light
Shine faith, and truth, and prayer;
And through the changing scenes of life,
I find a haven there.

AUTHOR UNKNOWN.

## MOTHER O' MINE

If I were hanged on the highest hill,
*Mother o' mine, O mother o' mine!*
I know whose love would follow me still,
*Mother o' mine, O mother o' mine!*
If I were drowned in the deepest sea,
*Mother o' mine, O mother o' mine!*
I know whose tears would come down to me,
*Mother o' mine, O mother o' mine!*
If I were damned by body and soul,
I know whose prayers would make me whole,
*Mother o' mine, O mother o' mine!*

RUDYARD KIPLING.

## LOVE'S TRIBUTE

I wear a snow white rose today
  In sacred memory,
In silent tribute to the love
  My mother bore for me.

The fairest flower will fade and die,
  But deeds live on for aye;
A life well lived shows proof of love
  Far more than words we say.

So I would live from day to day
  That all my life shall be
A living tribute to that love—
  A faithful memory.

LORENA W. STURGEON.

## A MOTHER'S NAME

No painter's brush, nor poet's pen
  In justice to her fame
Has ever reached half high enough
  To write a mother's name.

AUTHOR UNKNOWN.

## MOTHER

Each day to her a miracle,
  Fresh from her Father's hand;
She bore with patience every grief
  She could not understand.

The ears of others were her own,
  Their joys of hers a part;
The lonely never were alone
  Close to her tender heart.

No more along life's rugged path
  Her tired feet must roam,
For she, who made of home a Heaven,
  Wakes—to find Heaven her home!

AUTHOR UNKNOWN.

# MEMORIAL DAY

# MEMORIAL DAY

## MEMORIAL DAY

I heard a cry in the night from a far-flung host,
From a host that sleeps through the years the last long
sleep,
By the Meuse, by the Marne, in the Argonne's shattered
wood,
In a thousand rose-thronged churchyards through our
land.
Sleeps! Do they sleep! I know I heard their cry,
Shrilling along the night like a trumpet blast:

"We died," they cried, "for a dream. Have ye forgot?
We dreamed of a world reborn whence wars had fled,
Where swords were broken in pieces and guns were rust,
Where the poor man dwelt in quiet, the rich in peace,
And children played in the streets, joyous and free.
We thought we could sleep content in a task well done;
But the rumble of guns rolls over us, iron upon iron
Sounds from the forge where are fashioned guns anew;

New fleets spring up in new seas, and under the wave
Stealthy new terrors swarm, with emboweled death.
Fresh cries of hate ring out loud from the demagogue's
throat,
While greed reaches out afresh to grasp new lands.
Have we died in vain? Is our dream denied?
You men who live on the earth we bought with our woe,

Will ye stand idly by while they shape new wars,
Or will ye rise, who are strong, to fulfill our dream,
To silence the demagogue's voice, to crush the fools
Who play with blood-stained toys that crowd new graves?
We call, we call in the night, will ye hear and heed?"

In the name of our dead will we hear? Will we grant them sleep?

WILLIAM E. BROOKS.

## UNKNOWN SOLDIER

Flowers for you, O Glory's Son, War's prey!
How long, how long since you were laid
To guarded rest where a nation's shrine is made!
Nor care nor fighting touch you there.

A pretty spot, Soldier, above your head,
But you, brave Lad, are dead . . . are dead.
And in this world you gallantly forswore
Already leer and snarl the wolves of War,
While Folly, Hatred, Lust and Greed
Contend much as before.

Courage and the high heart were yours.
Then shall we patriots supinely heap
Your tomb with wreaths of fame
(Your price for Peace now half forgot), and weep
Old tears that Hero is your only name

We know? Nay, Lad! We valiant rise to keep
The faith with you and all youth, lest War number
All lovely things of life and dear
With sons he's sent to fatal slumber!

ALTA BOOTH DUNN.

## THE REDDENED ROAD

What of the empires that are built on beds of dead men's bones,
What of the piles of princely pomp, the palaces and thrones?
With none to blow the bugle blast to call the dogs of war,
Who then would mark to murder those they never met before?

One peasant lad, who plows the fields where grows the golden corn,
Is nobler breed than all the whelps the wolves of war have borne,
One song sung by some genial soul along some sheltered glade
Shall hush some day the savage shock that warrior's guns have made.

One gleam of love that suckling babe in mother's eyes beheld
Shall silence yet the threats of doom that tyrant's hate has yelled;

One word of brotherhood and peace, one breath of
    fragrant flowers,
These be the things of truest worth in this old world
    of ours.

H. M. Tickener.

## FAR AWAY FROM FLANDERS FIELD

In Flanders Fields the poppies grow
Beneath the crosses, row on row,
  Where comrades lie.
Now far away from Flanders Fields
On iron beds, in chairs with wheels,
  We fight or die.

We are the maimed. Twelve years ago
By gas or shell were we laid low
  On distant shores.
And then a new fight we began—
A fight 'gainst unseen foes of man
  In countless scores.

Keep up our fight 'gainst all that's base,
And make this world a better place
  In which to live.
If ye break faith with us who fell,
Ye spurn the life which we, when well,
  Did seek to give.

L. S. Uphoff.

## PEACE ON EARTH

The men of the earth said: "We must war
As the men of the earth have warred;
'Tis ours to wield on the battlefield
The unrelenting sword."
*But they who had seen the valiant die,*
*The fathers of men, they answered, "Why?"*

The men of the earth said: "We must arm,
For so we would reveal
The nobler part of the human heart,
The love of the nation's weal."
*But they who had sung their lullaby,*
*The mothers of men, they answered, "Why?"*

Then men of the earth said: "We must fight,
For so the fit survive;
By the jungle law of fang and claw
The strong are kept alive."
*But a crippled, cankered progeny,*
*The sons of the culls, they answered, "Why?"*

The men of the earth said: "We must fall,
And falling build the road
O'er which the race with quickening pace
Can find its way to God."
*But down from a Cross uplifted high,*
*The Saviour of men, He answered, "Why?"*

ROBERT FREEMAN.

## MEMORIAL DAY

A day of tender memory,
  A day of sacred hours,
Of little bands of marching men,
  Of drums and flags and flowers.

A day when a great nation halts
  Its mighty, throbbing pace,
It pays its meed of gratitude
  And love with willing grace.

A day when battles are retold,
  And eulogies are said,
When dirges sound, and chaplains read
  The office for the dead.

A day when fairest, sweetest blooms
  Are laid upon each grave,
And wreaths are hung on monuments,
  And banners, half-mast, wave.

A day to keep from year to year
  In memory of the dead;
Let music sound, and flowers be laid
  Upon each resting-bed.

EMMA A. LENT.

## MEMORIAL DAY

To all the heart-wounds touched afresh this day
  As on the Soldier's resting place we lay
Thy flowers, Christ, in tender memory,
  Give healing thou,
    This eventide.

And for the sorrowing ones who yet remain,
  To whom the heart-break and the bitter pain
Come like the memory of an old song's sad refrain,
  Have pity thou,
    This eventide.

For all the losses of the lonely years—
  For all the weight of shed and unshed tears,
For all forebodings, and all coming fears,
  Give quietness,
    This eventide.

By all the flower of youth in battle slain,
  By all the woman's heritage of pain;
The prayer that it may not have been in vain.
  We leave with thee,
    This eventide.

EVERETTE H. DUNNING.

## LITTLE GREEN TENTS

Little green tents where the soldiers sleep,
And the sunbeams play, and the women weep,
Are covered with flowers today;

And between the tents walk the weary few,
Who were young and stalwart in sixty-two
When they went to the war away.

The little green tents are built of sod,
And they are not long, and they are not broad,
But the soldiers have lots of room;
And the sod is a part of the land they saved,
When the flag of the enemy darkly waved,
The symbol of dole and doom.

The little green tent is a thing divine;
The little green tent is a country's shrine,
Where patriots kneel and pray.
And the brave men left, so old, so few,
Were young and stalwart in sixty-two,
When they went to the war away.

WALT MASON.

## THE NEW MEMORIAL DAY

"Under the roses the blue;
Under the lilies the gray."

Oh, the roses we plucked for the blue,
And the lilies we twined for the gray,
We have bound in a wreath,
And in silence beneath
Slumber our heroes today.

## MEMORIAL DAY

Over the new-turned sod
  The sons of our fathers stand,
And the fierce old fight
Slips out of sight
  In the clasp of a brother's hand.

For the old blood left a stain
  That the new has washed away,
And the sons of those
That have faced as foes
  Are marching together today.

Oh, the blood that our fathers gave!
  Oh, the tide of our mothers' tears!
And the flow of red,
And the tears they shed,
  Embittered a sea of years.

But the roses we plucked for the blue,
  And the lilies we twined for the gray
We have bound in a wreath,
And in glory beneath
  Slumber our heroes today.

ALBERT BIGELOW PAINE.

# FLAG DAY

# FLAG DAY

## YOUR FLAG AND MY FLAG

Your flag and my flag,
  And how it flies today,
In your land and my land,
  And half a world away!

Rose-red and blood-red,
  The stripes forever gleam;
Snow-white and soul-white—
  The good forefather's dream;
Sky-blue and true-blue,
  With stars to gleam aright—
The gloried guidon of the day;
  A shelter through the night.

Your flag and my flag!
  To every star and stripe
The drums beat as hearts beat
  And fifers shrilly pipe!
Your flag and my flag—
  A blessing in the sky;
Your hope and my hope—
  It never hid a lie!
Home land and far land
  And half the world around,
Old Glory hears our glad salute
  And ripples to the sound.

Your flag and my flag!
  And, Oh! how much it holds—
Your land and my land—
  Secure within its folds!
Your heart and my heart
  Beat quicker at the sight.
Sun-kissed and wind-tossed—
  Red and blue and white.
The one flag—the great flag—
  The flag for me and you
Glorified all else beside,
  The red and white and blue.

WILBUR D. NESBIT.

## THE FLAG GOES BY

Hats off!
Along the street there comes
A blare of bugles, a ruffle of drums,
A flash of color beneath the sky.
Hats off!
The flag is passing by!

Blue, and crimson, and white it shines,
Over the steel-tipped, ordered lines.
Hats off!
The colors before us fly;
But more than the flag is passing by.

Sea fights and land fights, grim and great,
Fought to make and to save the state;

## FLAG DAY

Weary marches and sinking ships;
Cheers of victory on dying lips;

Days of plenty, and years of peace,
March of a strong land's swift increase;
Equal justice, right, and law,
Stately honor and reverend awe;

Sign of a Nation, great and strong,
To ward her people from foreign wrong;
Pride, and glory, and honor, all
Live in the colors to stand or fall.

Hats off!
Along the street there comes
A blare of bugles, a ruffle of drums;
And loyal hearts are beating high.
Hats off!
The flag is passing by!

H. H. BENNETT.

## THE STAR-SPANGLED BANNER

O say, can you see, by the dawn's early light,
What so proudly we hailed at the twilight's last gleaming?
Whose broad stripes and bright stars, through the perilous fight,
O'er the ramparts we watched, were so gallantly streaming!
And the rockets' red glare, the bombs bursting in air,

Gave proof through the night that our flag was still
there:
O say, does that star-spangled banner yet wave
O'er the land of the free and the home of the brave?

On the shore, dimly seen through the mists of the deep,
Where the foe's haughty host in dread silence reposes,
What is that which the breeze, o'er the towering steep,
As it fitfully blows, now conceals, now discloses?
Now it catches the gleam of the morning's first beam,
In full glory reflected now shines on the stream:
'Tis the star-spangled banner! O long may it wave
O'er the land of the free and the home of the brave!

O! thus be it ever, when freemen shall stand
Between their loved homes and the war's desolation!
Blest with victory and peace, may the heaven-rescued
land
Praise the Power that hath made and preserved us a
nation.
Then conquer we must, for our cause it is just,
And this be our motto: "In God is our trust."
And the star-spangled banner in triumph shall wave
O'er the land of the free and the home of the brave!

FRANCIS SCOTT KEY.

## OLD FLAG FOREVER

She's up there,—Old Glory—where lightnings are sped;
She dazzles the nations with ripples of red;
And she'll wave for us living, or droop o'er us dead—
The flag of our country forever!

## FLAG DAY

She's up there,—Old Glory—how bright the stars stream!
And the stripes like red signals of liberty gleam!
And we dare for her, living, or dream the last dream,
'Neath the flag of our country forever!

She's up there,—Old Glory—no tyrant-dealt scars,
No blur on her brightness, no stain on her stars!
The brave blood of heroes hath crimsoned her bars.
She's the flag of our country forever!

FRANK L. STANTON.

## SALUTE THE FLAG

Off with your hat as the flag goes by!
  And let the heart have its say:
You're man enough for a tear in your eye
  That you will not wipe away.

You're man enough for a thrill that goes
  To your very finger-tips—
Ay! the lump just then in your throat that rose
  Spoke more than your parted lips.

Lift up the boy on your shoulder high,
  And show him the faded shred;
Those stripes would be red as the sunset sky
  If death could have dyed them red.

Off with your hat as the flag goes by!
  Uncover the youngster's head;
Teach him to hold it holy and high
  For the sake of its sacred dead.

H. C. BUNNER.

## OUR FLAG

Only a bit of color
  Waving upon the street;
Only a wind-whipped pennant
  Where the band plays shrill and sweet.

Yet the soldier's heart beats faster,
  And proud is the sailor's eye,
And the citizen's step is quickened
  When our flag is passing by.

Only a bit of color,
  Did I hear a body say?
True be the hearts that greet it
  Wherever it waves today!

Back of that bit of color
  Lies a nation's history,
And ahead of our splendid banner—
  Who knows what there yet may be?

FRANCES CROSBY HAMLET.

## I AM THE FLAG

I am a composite being of all the people of America.
I am the union if you are united.
I am one and indivisible if you are undivided.
I am as strong as the weakest link.
I am an emblem of your country.
I am a symbol of a shadow of the real.
I am a sign pointing to past achievements.

I am a promise of greater things for the future.
I am what you make me.
I am purity if you are pure.
I am bravery if you are brave.
I am loyalty if you are loyal.
I am prosperity if you are prosperous.
I am honor if you are honorable.
I am goodness if you are good.
I am hope if you are hopeful.
I am truth if you are true. I have not always been truth, for you were not always true. You boasted of the "land of the free and the home of the brave" when your boast was a half lie.
I was deceived because you deceived yourselves.
I am the Constitution.
I am law and order.
I am tolerance or intolerance as you force me to be.
I am liberty as you understand liberty.
I am as a pillar of fire by night, but you must provide the fuel.
I march at the head of the column, but you must carry me on.
I have marched across the continent from ocean to ocean during my young life, and watched the growth of a nation from fewer than three million to more than one hundred million, because you encouraged and forced me to do so.
I stand for greater and more glorious achievement than can be found in recorded history, but you must be my inspiration.
I AM THE FLAG.

LAWRENCE M. JONES.

# INDEPENDENCE DAY

# INDEPENDENCE DAY

## LOVE OF COUNTRY

Breathes there a man with soul so dead
Who never to himself hath said:
"This is my own, my native land"?
Whose heart hath ne'er within him burned
As home his footsteps he hath turned,
From wandering on a foreign strand?
If such there breathe, go mark him well;
For him no minstrel raptures swell;
High though his titles, proud his name,
Boundless his wealth as wish can claim,
Despite those titles, power and pelf,
The wretch concentered all in self,
Living, shall forfeit fair renown,
And, doubly dying, shall go down
To the vile dust from whence he sprung,
Unwept, unhonored, and unsung.

SIR WALTER SCOTT.

## TO OUR FOREFATHERS

You who have handed us life's torch, new kindled,
  We are your own, in us you live again.
Oh, may we prove your influence has not dwindled,
  That earth holds yet a sturdy race of men!

You who have given us all that we cherish—
  Life, and the gracious gifts that living brings—
Amid the trivial things that daily perish,
  Your spirit lifts us up to fairer things.

We are your children—citizens or sages,
  Sharing your race, your likeness, thought and aim:
Guarding life's spark, to hand it down the ages,
  And make earth somehow fairer that we came.

The swift years pass. Yet how should we forget you,
  Long gone before us, journeying on ahead?
We mold the eager dreams you left unfinished,
  Ere we must follow you whom men call dead.

God, make us worthy of the lives that shaped us!
  May our work stand when we have gone our way:
When, in the far-off years we shall not enter,
  Our children's children keep a hero's day.

FRANCES CROSBY HAMLET.

## I AM AN AMERICAN

"I am an American.
My father belongs to the Sons of the Revolution.
My mother to the Colonial Dames.
One of my ancestors pitched tea overboard in Boston harbor,
Another stood his ground with Warren,
Another hungered with Washington at Valley Forge.
My ancestors were Americans in the making.

They spoke in her council-halls,
They died on her battle-ships,
They cleared her forests.
Dawns reddened and paled.
Stanch hearts of mine beat fast at each new star
In the nation's flag.
Keen eyes of mine foresaw her greater glory—
The sweep of her seas,
The plenty of her plains,
The man-hives of her billion-wired cities.
Every drop of blood in me holds a heritage of patriotism.
I am an American!"

Then the Russian Jew speaks—
"I am an American.
My father was an atom of dust,
My mother a straw in the wind,
To His Serene Majesty.
One of my ancestors died in the mines of Siberia,
Another was crippled for life by twenty blows of the knout,
Another was killed defending his home during the massacres.
The history of my ancestors is a trail of blood
To the palace gates of the Great White Czar.
But then the dream came—
The dream of America.
In the light of the Liberty torch
The atom of dust became a man,
And the straw in the wind became a woman,
For the first time.

'See,' said my father, pointing to the flag that fluttered
near,
'That flag of stars and stripes is yours.
It is the emblem of the Promised Land.
It means, my son, the hope of humanity.
Live for it, die for it.'
Under the open sky of my new country
I swore to do so,
And every drop of blood in me
Will keep that vow.
I am proud of my future.
I am an American!"

ELIAS LIEBERMANN.

## *From* THE SHIP OF STATE

Thou, too, sail on, O ship of State!
Sail on, O Union, strong and great!
Humanity with all its fears,
With all its hopes of future years,
Is hanging breathless on thy fate!
We know what Master laid thy keel,
What workmen wrought thy ribs of steel,
Who made each mast, and sail, and rope,
What anvils rang, what hammers beat,
In what a forge and what a heat
Were shaped the anchors of thy hope!
Fear not each sudden sound and shock,
'Tis of the wave and not the rock;
'Tis but the flapping of the sail,
And not a rent made by the gale!

In spite of rock and tempest's roar,
In spite of false lights on the shore,
Sail on, nor fear to breast the sea!
Our hearts, our hopes, are all with thee,
Our hearts, our hopes, our prayers, our tears,
Our faith, triumphant o'er our fears,
Are all with thee—are all with thee!

HENRY WADSWORTH LONGFELLOW.

## *From* THE PRESENT CRISIS

When a deed is done for Freedom, through the broad earth's aching breast
Runs a thrill of joy prophetic, trembling on from east to west,
And the slave, where'er he cowers, feels the soul within him climb
To the awful verge of manhood, as the energy sublime
Of a century bursts full-blossomed on the thorny stem of Time.
New occasions teach new duties; Time makes ancient good uncouth;
They must upward still, and onward, who would keep abreast of Truth;
Lo, before us gleam her camp-fires! we ourselves must Pilgrims be,
Launch our Mayflower, and steer boldly through the desperate winter sea,
Nor attempt the Future's portal with the Past's blood-rusted key.

JAMES RUSSELL LOWELL.

## OUR COUNTRY

O Beautiful, my Country!
  Be thine a nobler care
Than all thy wealth of commerce,
  Thy harvests waving fair:
Be it thy pride to lift up
  The manhood of the poor;
Be thou to the oppressed
  Fair Freedom's open door!

For thee our fathers suffered,
  For thee they toiled and prayed;
Upon thy holy altar
  Their willing lives they laid.
Thou hast no common birthright,
  Grand memories on thee shine;
The blood of pilgrim nations
  Commingled, flows in thine.

O Beautiful, our Country!
  Round thee in love we draw:
Thine is the grace of Freedom,
  The majesty of Law.
Be Righteousness thy sceptre,
  Justice thy diadem;
And on thy shining forehead
  Be Peace the crowning gem!

FREDERICK L. HOSMER.

## AMERICA THE BEAUTIFUL

O beautiful for spacious skies,
For amber waves of grain,
For purple mountain majesties
Above the fruited plain!
America! America!
God shed his grace on thee
And crown thy good with brotherhood
From sea to shining sea!

O beautiful for pilgrim feet,
Whose stern, impassioned stress
A thoroughfare for freedom beat
Across the wilderness!
America! America!
God mend thine every flaw,
Confirm thy soul in self-control,
Thy liberty in law!

O beautiful for heroes proved
In liberating strife,
Who more than self their country loved,
And mercy more than life!
America! America!
May God thy gold refine
Till all success be nobleness
And every gain divine!

O beautiful for patriot dream
That sees beyond the years

Thine alabaster cities gleam
Undimmed by human tears!
America! America!
God shed His grace on thee
And crown thy good with brotherhood
From sea to shining sea!

KATHARINE LEE BATES.

## THE LAND WHERE HATE SHOULD DIE

This is the land where hate should die—
No feuds of faith, no spleen of race,
No darkly brooding fear should try
Beneath our flag to find a place.
Lo! every people here has sent
Its sons to answer freedom's call;
Their lifeblood is the strong cement
That builds and binds the nation's wall.

This is the land where hate should die—
Though dear to me my faith and shrine,
I serve my country well when I
Respect beliefs that are not mine.
He little loves his land who'd cast
Upon his neighbor's word a doubt,
Or cite the wrongs of ages past
From present rights to bar him out.

This is the land where hate should die—
This is the land where strife should cease,
Where foul, suspicious fear should fly
Before our flag of light and peace.

Then let us purge from poisoned thought
That service to the state we give,
And so be worthy as we ought
Of this great land in which we live!

DENIS A. McCARTHY.

## THEY TELL ME THOU ART RICH

They tell me thou art rich, my country: gold
In glittering flood has poured into thy chest;
Thy flocks and herds increase; thy barns are pressed
With harvest, and thy stores can hardly hold
Their merchandise; unending trains are rolled
Along thy network rails of east and west;
Thy factories and forges never rest;
Thou art enriched in all things bought and sold!
But dost thou prosper? Better news I crave.

O Dearest Country, is it well with thee
Indeed, and is thy soul in health?
A nobler people, hearts more wisely brave,
And thoughts that lift men up and make them free—
These are prosperity and vital wealth!

AUTHOR UNKNOWN.

## AMERICA GREETS AN ALIEN

Hail guest! We ask not what thou art.
If friend, we greet thee hand and heart;
If stranger, such no longer be;
If foe, our love shall conquer thee.

AUTHOR UNKNOWN.

## PATRIOTISM

He serves his country best
Who lives pure life and doeth righteous deed,
And walks straight paths however others stray,
And leaves his sons, as uttermost bequest,
A stainless record which all men may read;
This is the better way.

No drop but serves the slowly lifting tide;
No dew but has an errand to some flower;
No smallest star but sheds some helpful ray,
And man by man, each helping all the rest,
Make the firm bulwark of the country's power;
There is no better way.

SUSAN COOLIDGE.

## THE STARS AND STRIPES

Thank God we can see, in the glory of morn
The invincible flag that our fathers defended;
And our hearts can repeat what the heroes have sworn,
That war shall not end till the war-lust is ended.
Then the blood-thirsty sword shall no longer be lord
Of the nations oppressed by the conqueror's horde,
But the banners of freedom shall peacefully wave
Over the world of the free and the lands of the brave.

HENRY VAN DYKE.

# LABOR DAY

# LABOR DAY

## NOBLE WORK

Who lags from dread of daily work,
And his appointed task would shirk,
  Commits a folly and a crime:
    A soulless slave—
    A paltry knave—
  A clog upon the wheels of time,
With work to do, and store of health,
  The man's unworthy to be free,
    Who will not give,
    That he may live,
  His daily toil for daily fee.

No! Let us work! We only ask
Reward proportion'd to our task;
  We have no quarrel with the great—
    No feud with rank—
    With mill or bank—
  No envy of a lord's estate.
If we can earn sufficient store
  To satisfy our daily need,
    And can retain,
    For age and pain,
  A fraction, we are rich indeed.

No dread of toil have we or ours;
We know our worth, and weigh our powers;
The more we work, the more we win;
Success to trade!
Success to spade!
And to the corn that's coming in!
And joy to him who o'er his task
Remembers toil is Nature's plan;
Who, working, thinks,
And never sinks
His independence as a man!

CHARLES MACKAY.

## THE DAY AND THE WORK

To each man is given a day and his work for the day;
And once, and no more, he is given to travel this way.
And woe if he flies from the task, whatever the odds;
For the task is appointed to him on the scroll of the gods.

There is waiting a work where only your hands can avail;
And so, if you falter, a chord in the music will fail.
We may laugh to this sky, we may lie for an hour in the sun;
But we dare not go hence till the labor appointed is done.

To each man is given a marble to carve for the wall;
A stone that is needed to heighten the beauty of all;
And only his soul has the magic to give it a grace;
And only his hands have the cunning to put it in place.

## LABOR DAY

We are given one hour to parley and struggle with Fate,
Our wild hearts filled with the dream, our brains with
the high debate.
It is given to look on life once, and once only to die:
One testing, and then at a sign we go out of the sky.

Yes, the task that is given to each man, no other can do;
So your work is awaiting: it has waited through ages
for you.
And now you appear, and the Husht Ones are turning
their gaze
To see what to do with your chance in the chamber
of days.

EDWIN MARKHAM.

## THE GOSPEL OF LABOR

This is the Gospel of Labor—
Ring it, ye bells of the kirk—
The Lord of love came down from above
To live with the men who work.
This is the rose that he planted
Here in the thorn cursed soil—
Heaven is blessed with perfect rest;
But the blessing of earth is toil.

HENRY VAN DYKE.

## MY SONG

Lord let me work! At singing I have failed.
My silly word-bound lips cannot release
The turbulence of song that finds no peace

But smolders in my heart, a force impaled.
Oh let me work that somehow in the sweat
Of groaning loins . . . of straining thews . . . and
strife . . .
There in the grim realities of life,
In all the filth and grime, the cold and wet,
My song, at last, may find itself expressed.
It will not soar as do the songs of those,
Who better blessed than I, in words disclose
Their inner fires, their groping souls' unrest.
Lord let me work, and working build my song
And may I shape it firm and clean and strong.

EUNICE K. BIDDLE.

## SONG OF CHRISTIAN WORKINGMEN

Our Master toiled, a carpenter
Of busy Galilee;
He knew the weight of ardent tasks
And ofttimes, wearily,
He sought, apart, in earnest prayer
For strength, beneath His load of care.

He took a manly share of work,
No thoughtless shirker He.
From dawn to dusk, before His bench,
He labored faithfully.
He felt just pride in work well done
And found rest sweet, at setting sun.

His Father worked, and He rejoiced
That honest toil was His

To whom was given grace to know
  Divinest mysteries:
And shall not we find toiling good
Who serve in labor's brotherhood?

THOMAS CURTIS CLARK.

## THE MASTER OF LABORERS

O Master of the common weal,
The shop, the field, the market place!
Thou knowest all the pangs we feel.
Thou knowest all our need of grace;
And where the world's injustice goads
The weary, on the climbing roads,
Stoop once again with tender voice,
Though clanging discord fills the air,
To whisper hope and bid rejoice
All who the world's oppression bear.
O Master of the toiling clan,
Thou Son of God! Thou Son of Man!

GEORGE EDWARD DAY.

## THE MASTER'S MAN

My Master was a worker
  With daily work to do,
And he who would be like Him
  Must be a worker, too;
Then welcome honest labor
  And honest labor's fare,
For where there is a worker
  The Master's man is there.

My Master was a comrade,
  A trusty friend and true,
And he who would be like Him
  Must be a comrade too;
In happy hours of singing,
  In silent hours of care,
Where goes a loyal comrade,
  The Master's man is there.

My Master was a helper,
  The woes of life He knew,
And he who would be like Him
  Must be a helper too;
The burden will grow lighter,
  If each will take a share,
And where there is a helper
  The Master's man is there.

Then, brothers, brave and manly,
  Together let us be,
For He, who is our Master,
  The Man of men was He;
The men who would be like Him
  Are wanted everywhere,
And where they love each other
  The Master's men are there.

WILLIAM G. TARRANT.

## ARISTOCRATS OF LABOR

They claim no guard of heraldry,
They scorn the knightly rod;
Their coats of arms are noble deeds,
Their peerage is from God!

W. Stewart.

## WORK

Work thou for pleasure.
Paint or sing or carve
The thing thou lovest,
Though the body starve.
Who works for glory
Misses oft the goal,
Who works for money
Coins his very soul.
Work for the work's sake,
Then, and it might be
That these things shall
Be added unto thee.

Kenyon Cox.

## THE LABORER

Back to the sun he ploughed the mead,
As evening's conflagration
Burnt up the hill, and could not heed
His own transfiguration.

Evan Thomas.

# ARMISTICE DAY

# ARMISTICE DAY

## "THIS IS THE LAST"

Coming in splendor thro' the golden gate
Of all the days, swift passing, one by one,
O silent planet, thou hast gazed upon
How many harvestings dispassionate?
Across the many-furrowed fields of Fate,
Wrapt in the mantle of oblivion,
The old, gray, wrinkled Husbandman has gone;
The blare of trumpets, rattle of the drum,
Disturb him not at all—he sees,
Between the hedges of the centuries,
A thousand phantom armies go and come,
While reason whispers as each marches past,
"This is the last of wars—this is the last!"

GILBERT WATERHOUSE.

## THE NEW SONG

Poet, take up thy lyre;
No more shall warlike fire
  Inflame the earth and sea;
Cease from your martial strain,
Sing songs of peace again,
  Sing of a world set free.

No more sing fear and hate
While armies devastate,
 Nor boast of foes withstood;
Let mercy be your theme,
Renew the old, fair dream
 Of human brotherhood.

No more the trumpet blast
Shall call to conflict fast,
 The flame of war grows pale;
Sing, Poet, God-inspired,
Till all the world is fired
 With love that shall not fail.

ARTHUR GORDON FIELD.

## THE VISION OF PEACE

O, beautiful Vision of Peace,
 Beam bright in the eyes of Man!
The host of the meek shall increase,
 The Prophets are leading the van.
Have courage; we see the Morn!
 Never fear, though the Now be dark!
Out of Night the Day is born;
 The Fire shall live from the Spark.

It may take a thousand years
 Ere the Era of Peace holds sway,
Look back and the Progress cheers,
 And a thousand years are a day!

## ARMISTICE DAY

The World grows—yet not by chance;
  It follows some marvelous plan;
Tho' slow to our wish the advance,
  God rules the training of Man.

NATHAN HASKELL DOLE.

## BUGLE SONG OF PEACE

Blow, bugle, blow!
  The day has dawned at last,
Blow, blow, blow!
  The fearful night is past;
The prophets realize their dreams.
Lo! in the east the glory gleams.
Blow, bugle, blow!
The day has dawned at last.

Blow, bugle, blow!
  The soul of man is free.
The rod and sword of king and lord
  Shall no more honored be;
For God alone shall govern men,
And Love shall come to earth again.
Blow, bugle, blow!
The soul of man is free.

Blow, bugle, blow!
  Though rivers run with blood,
All greed and strife, and lust for life,
  Are passing with the flood.

The gory beast of war is cowed;
The world's great heart with grief is bowed.
Blow, bugle, blow!
The day has dawned at last!

THOMAS CURTIS CLARK.

## "NEXT TIME"

The order goes; what if we rush ahead
With friendly shouts—with welcoming and cheer
And loyal clasp of fellowship—instead
Of lethal gas, and bombs that maim and sear—
"Next time"?

If, in accord, the armies look afar
Where droops a Figure on a Cross; and hear,
"Of all my woe, ye make a mockery!"
With Him allied—what cause have we to fear—
"Next time"?

Firm in our faith, we stand together there—
Comrades and brothers; if we must be slain
So let our captains take us; but Beware!
*They cannot make us ope His wounds again*—
"Next time"!

LAURA SIMMONS.

## *From* TEN YEARS AFTER

The old world staggers, but a young, triumphant world
is born.
Before the Tower of Babel, sound a clear, resurgent horn
And prophesy the jubilant dawn when a true peace will
come!
Make the will of the world your trumpet, the heart of
the world your drum!

RALPH CHEYNEY.

## ARMISTICE

We face the nations with one hand outstretched
In greeting, and with peace upon our lips;
But in our hearts a question, in our minds
The haunting echoes of the song of war,
The song that sets the world a-tremble still
And shakes the very pillars of our faith.

How long before the peace can pass our lips,
Can claim our minds and drive out old distrust?
To doubt mankind is but to doubt ourselves.
When shall our fingers dare to drop the sword,
While with unquestioning eyes we reach two hands
In open comradeship to all the world?

EUNICE MITCHELL LEHMER.

## THE MESSAGE OF PEACE

Bid the din of battle cease!
Folded be the wings of fire!
Let your courage conquer peace—
Every gentle heart's desire.

Let the crimson flood retreat!
Blended in the arc of love,
Let the flags of nations meet;
Bind the raven, loose the dove;

At the altar that we raise
King and Kaiser may bow down;
Warrior-knights above their bays
Wear the sacred olive crown.

Blinding passion is subdued,
Men discern their common birth,
God hath made of kindred blood
All the peoples of the earth.

High and holy are the gifts
He has lavished on the race—
Hope that quickens, prayer that lifts,
Honor's meed, and beauty's grace.

As in Heaven's bright face we look
Let our kindling souls expand;
Let us pledge, on nature's book,
Heart to heart and hand to hand.

## ARMISTICE DAY

For the glory that we saw
 In the battle-flag unfurled,
Let us read Christ's better law:
 Fellowship for all the world!

JULIA WARD HOWE.

## 1914—AND AFTER

Would you end war?
Create great Peace. . . .

The Peace that demands all of a man,
His love, his life, his veriest self;
Plunge him into the smelting fires of a work that becomes his child,

Give him a hard Peace; a Peace of discipline and justice. . . .
Kindle him with vision, invite him to joy and adventure;
Set him to work, not to create *things*,
But to create *man;*
Yea, himself.

Go, search your heart, America . . .
Turn from the machine to man,
Build, while there is yet time, a creative Peace. . . .

While there is yet time!
For if you reject great Peace,
As surely as vile living brings disease,
So surely will your selfishness bring war.

JAMES OPPENHEIM.

## GRASS

Pile the bodies high at Austerlitz and Waterloo,
Shovel them under and let me work—
  I am the grass; I cover all.

And pile them high at Gettysburg,
  And pile them high at Ypres and Verdun,
Shovel them under and let me work.
Two years, ten years, and passengers ask the conductor:
  What place is this?
  Where are we now?

  I am the grass.
  Let me work.

CARL SANDBURG.

## THE END OF THE WORLD

I have been searching for the end of the world
Where all the flags and banners wildly unfurled
Have been placed in their racks and the noisy drums
Have ceased their beating, for the king who comes
With nothing but his presence to tell he is here.
I have been waiting for peace and rest to appear.

Somewhere—I know there must be a silent place
Where men choose only to behold the face
Of that strange king who needs no blatant herald.
Today the peace of a song bird has been imperiled
By drums and horns and noisy fanfarronade.
I am looking for peace before I meet my God.

## ARMISTICE DAY

I have laid my garments for princes, kings and queens
Whose only sceptres and crowns were cruel machines.
I have bowed to a god who could not last a year
And I bowed down before him in trembling and fear.
Lord, I am weary of the steel gods that break.
Show me the end of the world where silences wake.

RAYMOND KRESENSKY.

## THERE SHALL BE NEW SONGS

There will always be songs:
when the hearts of men are saddest
under the bludgeons of oppressors,
under the lash of masters,
under the threat of fire and steel
new songs come
to lift the courage of men.

The righteous have slain the gods,
they have broken the wine jars,
they have forbidden love.
Yet like smoke out of the ruins
songs rise
to keep alive the old joy under the long sorrow.

Song is mighty and deathless:
though the righteous drive men with whips to war,
though they break bodies and spirits in prison,
though they wield scorn that is stronger than guns and
prisons,
song is stronger than all the strength of the righteous;
they can not shatter song.

Still in the darkness men dream
of ways of comradely living;
still in the dungeons they cry
for the life-giving bread of freedom;
still in the morass of tradition
they climb toward the light.
Still in their songs the vision
is luminous and alive. It speaks:

"There shall be peace and brotherhood,
there shall be no poverty and no riches.
Men shall speak what they will, and their altars
be free, and they shall be free who have none.
There shall be freedom to live and love and be peaceful
and there shall be new songs . . ."

CLIFFORD GESSLER.

## WHEN WAR SHALL BE NO MORE

Were half the power that fills the world with terror,
  Were half the wealth bestowed on camps and courts,
Given to redeem the human mind from error,
  There were no need of arsenals and forts.

The warrior's name would be a name abhorrèd!
  And every nation, that should lift again
Its hand against a brother, on its forehead
  Would wear forevermore the curse of Cain!

Down the dark future, through long generations,
  The echoing sounds grow fainter and then cease;

And like a bell, with solemn, sweet vibrations,
  I hear once more the voice of Christ say, "Peace!"

Peace! and no longer from its brazen portals
  The blast of war's great organ shakes the skies!
But beautiful as the songs of the immortals,
  The holy melodies of Love arise.

HENRY WADSWORTH LONGFELLOW.

## LET THERE BE NO MORE BATTLES!

Yes, we would honor our heroic dead,
Would lay a wreath on each heroic head.
They all have perished for their dream of truth,
Died with the dare of youth.

They are not dead: life's flag is never furled:
They only passed on lightly, world to world.
Their bodies sleep, but in that Better Land
Their spirits march under a new command.

But there is something nobler yet—to live,
Live gallantly, to give and to forgive.
Yes, there is something nobler than all war—
To make our Country worth our dying for—
To lay the beams of Justice on the earth,
And call the Brother Future into birth.

This is a day that is dear,
A day when God is near—
The day when battles ended for a space:
Let it become the conscience of the race.

O sons of time and tears,
The skies are weary of these screaming shells,
The fields are weary of these battle hells:
Send a new vision of the coming years.
Set this great day as a holy day apart,
For dreams of Peace, the wisdom of the heart.
Yes, let this day, O men of earth, become
The dawn-rise of a new millennium.

O friends of Christ, this is our dream, for we
Must strive on toward the Brotherhood to be—
Toward that great hour of God's ascending sun
When all shall love and all shall lift as one.

EDWIN MARKHAM.

## PEACE

Not with the high-voiced fife,
  Nor with the deep-voiced drum,
To mark the end of strife
  The perfect Peace shall come.

Nor pomp nor pageant grand
  Shall bring War's blest surcease,
But silent, from God's hand
  Shall come the perfect Peace!

CLINTON SCOLLARD.

## IT SHALL NOT BE AGAIN!

Who goes there, in the night,
  Across the storm-swept plain?
*We are the ghosts of a valiant war—*
  *A million murdered men!*

Who goes there, at the dawn,
  Across the sun-swept plain?
*We are the hosts of those who swear;*
  *It shall not be again!*

THOMAS CURTIS CLARK.

## WHICH SWORD?

A sword, a sword, and a sword;
  Which sword will you draw, my Son?
For one is of steel with its blind appeal
  Till the folly of war is done.
'Tis an honor to fight for God and the right
  But justice is seldom won.

And one is the sword of truth,
  God's swift and naked blade
That puts to flight the lies of night
  And the hatred falsehoods made.
We are cowards all when lies appall,
  But in truth we are unafraid.

And one is a flaming sword
  Whose work is but begun;
Its glorious part is to change the heart,
  Its victories always won.
Draw this and smite with all thy might,—
  'Tis the sword of love, my Son.

JASON NOBLE PIERCE.

## TO FREEDOM

Freedom, not won by the vain,
  Not to be courted in play,
Not to be kept without pain.
  Stay with us! Yes, thou wilt stay,
Handmaid and mistress of all,
  Kindler of deed and of thought,
Thou that to hut and to hall
  Equal deliverance brought!
Souls of her martyrs, draw near,
  Touch our dull lips with your fire,
That we may praise without fear
  Her our delight, our desire,
Our faith's inextinguishable star,
Our hope, our remembrance, our trust,
  Our present, our past, our to be,
Who will mingle her life with our dust
  And make us deserve to be free!

JAMES RUSSELL LOWELL.

## CHRISTIANITY AND WAR

Talk, if you will, of hero deed,
  Of clash of arms and battle wonders;
But prate not of your Christian creed
  Preached by the cannon's murderous thunders.

And if your courage needs a test,
  Copy the pagan's fierce behavior;
Revel in bloodshed East and West,
  But speak not with it of the Saviour.

The Turk may wage a righteous war
  In honor of his martial Allah:
But Thor and Odin live no more—
  Dead are the Gods in our Valhalla.

Be what you will, entire and free,
  Christian or Warrior—each can please us;
But not the rank hypocrisy
  Of war-like followers of Jesus.

ERNEST CROSBY.

## THE HYMN OF HATE

And this I hate—not men, nor flag, nor race,
But only War with its wild, grinning face.
God strike it till its eyes be blind as night
And all its members tremble with affright!
Oh, let it hear in its death agony

The wail of mothers for their best-loved ones,
    And on its head
Descend the venomed curses of its sons
Who followed her, deluded, where its guns
    Had dyed the daisies red.

All these I hate—war and its panoply,
The lie that hides its ghastly mockery,
That makes its glories out of women's tears,
The toil of peasants through the burdened years,
The legacy of long disease that preys
On bone and body in the after-days.
    God's curses pour,
Until it shrivel with its votaries
And die away in its own fiery seas,
    That nevermore
Its dreadful call of murder may be heard;
A thing accursed in very deed and word
    From blood-drenched shore to shore!

JOSEPH DANA MILLER.

# THANKSGIVING DAY

# THANKSGIVING DAY

## THANKSGIVING

What art Thou saying, Lord, to me
By the red-fruited tree—
The yellow pumpkin on its frosted vine—
The purple grapes down by the old stone wall—
That tangle of late asters—silken corn-stalks tall—
Beauty of naked branches and a saffron sky,
That squadron of wild geese that southward fly?
Even the humble carrot hath an orange coat,
The beet a crimson robe—an onion silver skin.
By the rich walnut tree
I see the grey squirrel scampering, filling winter-bin.
The dainty weed beside the road doth yield
A perfect seed, wrought with divinest care;
Sometimes the wonder seems too great to bear.
Oh Lord, Thy beauteous bounty doth ensnare my soul!
I bow with great thanksgiving!

GENE H. OSBORNE.

## I THANK MY GOD——

Because in tender majesty,
Thou cam'st to earth nor stayed till we
Poor sinners stumbled up to Thee,
I thank my God.

Because the Saviour of us all
Lay with the cattle in their stall,
Because the Great comes to the small,
I thank my God.

Because upon a Mother's breast,
The Lord of Life was laid to rest,
And was of Babes the loveliest,
I thank my God.

Because the Eternal Infinite,
Was once that naked little mite,
Because, O Love, of Christmas night,
I thank my God.

G. A. STUDDERT-KENNEDY.

## THANK GOD!

Thank God for life!
E'en though it bring much bitterness and strife,
And all our fairest hopes be wrecked and lost,
E'en though there be more ill than good in life,
We cling to life and reckon not the cost.
Thank God for life!

Thank God for love!
For though sometimes grief follows in its wake,
Still we forget love's sorrow in love's joy,
And cherish tears with smiles for love's dear sake;
Only in heaven is bliss without lloy.
Thank God for love!

## THANKSGIVING DAY

Thank God for pain!
No tear hath ever yet been shed in vain,
And in the end each sorrowing heart shall find
No curse, but blessings in the hand of pain;
Even when He smiteth, then is God most kind.
Thank God for pain!

Thank God for death!
Who touches anguished lips and stills their breath
And giveth peace unto each troubled breast;
Grief flies before thy touch, O blessed death;
God's sweetest gift; thy name in heaven is Rest.
Thank God for death!

AUTHOR UNKNOWN.

## *From* A TE DEUM OF THE COMMONPLACE

For all the wonders of this wondrous world:
The pure pearl splendors of the coming day,
The breaking east—the rosy flush—the dawn,
For that bright gem in morning's coronal,
That one lone star that gleams above the glow;
For that high glory of the impartial sun—
The golden noonings big with promised life;
The matchless pageant of the evening skies,
The wide-flung gates—the gleams of Paradise,
Supremest visions of Thine artistry;
The sweet, soft gloaming, and the friendly stars;
The vesper stillness, and the creeping shades;
The moon's pale majesty; the pulsing dome,
Wherein we feel Thy great heart throbbing near;

For sweet laborious days and restful nights;
For work to do, and strength to do the work;
We thank Thee, Lord!

JOHN OXENHAM.

## PRAYER TO THE GIVER

Lord, I am glad for the great gift of living—
Glad for Thy days of sun and of rain;
Grateful for joy, with an endless thanksgiving,
Grateful for laughter—and grateful for pain.

Lord, I am glad for the young April's wonder,
Glad for the fulness of long summer days;
And now when the spring and my heart are asunder,
Lord, I give thanks for the dark autumn ways.

Sun, bloom, and blossom, O Lord, I remember,
The dream of the spring and its joy I recall;
But now in the silence and pain of November,
Lord, I give thanks to Thee, Giver of all!

CHARLES HANSON TOWNE.

## THANKS FOR NEW OPPORTUNITIES

Master divine,
We thank Thee for all new blessings,
For this new day
With its new opportunities of service for Thee and communion with Thee.
We thank Thee for landmarks passed

And new vistas opening ahead;
For new hope and new inspiration,
New national awakening, and new desire to serve our
time and our country.

We thank Thee that, to those who love Thee,
The best is ever yet to be:
That, if we abide in Thee, we can never grow old,
For Thou, our Master, art eternally young,
Eternally radiant with the joyful energy, the freshness
and buoyancy of youth.

We thank Thee for the sacred elixir of Thy Spirit,
Which wardeth forever from those who love Thee
All weariness of soul, all carking anxiety,
All discouragement in failure,
All old age of the soul.

*From* Prayers for Use in an Indian College.

## FATHER, WE THANK THEE

For flowers that bloom about our feet,
Father, we thank Thee,
For tender grass so fresh and sweet,
Father, we thank Thee,
For song of bird and hum of bee,
For all things fair we hear or see,
Father in heaven, we thank Thee.

For blue of stream and blue of sky,
Father, we thank Thee,
For pleasant shade of branches high,
Father, we thank Thee,

For fragrant air and cooling breeze,
For beauty of the blooming trees,
Father in heaven, we thank Thee.

For this new morning with its light,
Father, we thank Thee,
For rest and shelter of the night,
Father, we thank Thee,
For health and food, for love and friends,
For everything Thy goodness sends,
Father in heaven, we thank Thee.

RALPH WALDO EMERSON.

## HARVEST HYMN

Once more the liberal year laughs out
O'er richer stores than gems or gold;
Once more with harvest-song and shout
Is Nature's bloodless triumph told.

Oh, favors every year made new!
Oh, gifts with rain and sunshine sent!
The bounty overruns our due,
The fulness shames our discontent.

We shut our eyes, the flowers bloom on;
We murmur, but the corn-ears fill,
We choose the shadow, but the sun
That casts it shines behind us still.

Who murmurs at his lot today?
  Who scores his native fruit and bloom?
Or sighs for dainties far away,
  Beside the bounteous board of home?

Thank Heaven, instead, that Freedom's arm
  Can change a rocky soil to gold,—
That brave and generous lives can warm
  A clime with northern ices cold.

And let these altars, wreathed with flowers
  And piled with fruits, awake again
Thanksgivings for the golden hours,
  The early and the latter rain!

John Greenleaf Whittier.

## WE THANK THEE, LORD

We thank Thee, Lord,
For all Thy Golden Silences—
Silence of moorlands rolling to the skies,
Heath-purpled, bracken-clad, aflame with gorse;
Silence of deep woods' mystic cloistered calm;
Silence of wide seas basking in the sun;
Silence of white peaks soaring to the blue;
Silence of dawnings, when, their matins sung,
The little birds do fall asleep again;
For the deep silence of the golden noons;
Silence of gloamings and the setting sun;
Silence of moonlit nights and patterned glades;
Silence of stars, magnificently still,

Yet ever chanting their Creator's skill;
Deep unto deep, within us sound sweet chords
Of praise beyond the reach of human words;
In our souls' silence, feeling only Thee—
We thank Thee, thank Thee,
Thank Thee, Lord!

JOHN OXENHAM.

## A PRAYER

Give me work to do;
Give me health;
Give me joy in simple things.
Give me an eye for beauty,
A tongue for truth,
A heart that loves,
A mind that reasons,
A sympathy that understands;
Give me neither malice nor envy,
But a true kindness
And a noble common sense.
At the close of each day
Give me a book,
And a friend with whom
I can be silent.

AUTHOR UNKNOWN.

## I HAVE MY CRUSE OF OIL

I have my cruse of oil,
I have my cake of meal;
I am worn with life's long toil,

The threads are few on the reel.
One by one from the ranks fell out
The mates who joined them with cheer and shout,
When the merry march in the morn begun,
Under the laugh of the rising sun;
One by one they drop to the grave,
Where the pale stars gleam and the grasses wave;
On the surcoat is rent and soil,
The dents are deep on the steel,
Yet I have my cruse of oil,
I have my cake of meal.

WILLIAM WETMORE STORY.

*From* Tired.

## A ROAD SONG

These to be thankful for: a friend,
A work to do, a way to wend,
And these in which to take delight:
The wind that turns the poplars white,

Wonder and gleam of common things,
Sunlight upon a sea-gull's wings,
Odors of earth and dew-drenched lawns,
The pageantry of darks and dawns;

Blue vistas of a city street
At twilight, music, passing feet,
The thrill of Spring, half joy, half pain,
The deep voice of the Autumn rain.

Shall we not be content with these
Imperishable mysteries?
And jocund-hearted take our share
Of joy and pain and find life fair?—

Wayfarers on a road where we
Set forth each day right valiantly,
Expectant, dauntless, blithe, content,
To make the great experiment.

AUTHOR UNKNOWN.

## OUR PRAYER

Thou that hast given so much to me,
Give one thing more—a grateful heart;
Not thankful when it pleaseth me,
As if thy blessings had spare days;
But such a heart, whose pulse may be
Thy praise.

GEORGE HERBERT.

## A THANKSGIVING PRAYER

O, Thou, who hast comforted me in the night watches, Unto Thee I make my prayer, my prayer of thanksgiving:

For stars in every midnight sky,
For quivering glory in the grey,
For roses red—December grown,

## THANKSGIVING DAY

For sunset at the end of day.
For that swift turning back to Thee
In joy or sorrow, peace or pain,
For the frustration of my plans
That mine might be the greater gain.
For graveyards that no terror hold,
For death which is the mask of life,
For love unaltered by the years,
For heart at rest in midst of strife.
For that best gift of all, Thyself,
For Thy dear Presence shining through,
And for Thy grace, Thy boundless grace,
Accept, O Lord, my thanks anew,

As I, whom Thou hast comforted, in the night watches
Make unto Thee my prayer, my prayer of thanksgiving.

RUTH G. WINANT.

# CHRISTMAS

# CHRISTMAS

## THE WAY TO BETHLEHEM

Long was the way to Bethlehem
  To those who sought of old,
By burning sands and bitter springs
  And nights of haunting cold,
Bearing their nard and frankincense,
  Their precious gems and gold.

Hard was the way to Bethlehem,
  So far it seemed, so far,
By flowerless vales and arid slopes
  And barren heights that bar,
With ne'er an omen for a guide
  Until they saw the star.

But then the way to Bethlehem,
  It was no longer lone;
Joy was their comrade, those who trod
  O'er bruising shard and stone,
Until they found for king a Child,
  A manger for His throne.

Upon the way to Bethlehem,
  Till time shall bring release,
However dim and rough the path
  May not our footsteps cease,

Since at the end for us awaits
The guerdon of His peace!

CLINTON SCOLLARD.

## A PRAYER OF PENITENCE

Christ of the market, and the Christmas flare,
Be not too much distressed
That still our greeds invest
Remembrance of Thee with such gaudy wear.

Thou knowest that between the Christmas days—
Slowly—how slowly, Lord!—
We move to more accord
With what Thou willest for our common ways.

Bear with us yet, Christ of the dispossessed!
Christ of the lowly born!
Until earth's every morn
Shall see Thy love in all our lives confessed.

ROBERT WHITAKER.

## HOW FAR TO BETHLEHEM

"How far is it to Bethlehem town?"
Just over Jerusalem hills adown,
Past lovely Rachel's white-domed tomb—
Sweet shrine of motherhood's young doom.

It isn't far to Bethlehem town—
Just over the dusty roads adown,

## CHRISTMAS

Past Wise Men's well, still offering
Cool draughts from welcome wayside spring;
Past shepherds with their flutes of reed
That charm the woolly sheep they lead;
Past boys with kites on hilltops flying,
And soon you're there where Bethlehem's lying.
Sunned white and sweet on olived slopes,
Gold-lighted still with Judah's hopes.

And so we find the Shepherd's field
And plain that gave rich Boaz yield;
And look where Herod's villa stood.
We thrill that earthly parenthood
Could foster Christ who was all-good;
And thrill that Bethlehem town today
Looks down on Christmas homes that pray.

It isn't far to Bethlehem town!
It's anywhere that Christ comes down
And finds in people's friendly face
A welcome and abiding place.
The road to Bethlehem runs right through
The homes of folks like me and you.

MADELEINE SWEENY MILLER.

## CHRISTMAS BELLS

I heard the bells on Christmas Day
Their old familiar carols play,
And wild and sweet the words repeat
Of peace on earth, good will to men!

I thought how, as the day had come,
The belfries of all Christendom
Had rolled along the unbroken song
Of peace on earth, good will to men!

And in despair I bowed my head;
"There is no peace on earth," I said;
"For hate is strong, and mocks the song
Of peace on earth, good will to men."

Then pealed the bells more loud and deep:
"God is not dead, nor doth he sleep!
The wrong shall fail, the right prevail,
With peace on earth, good will to men!"

Till, ringing, singing on its way,
The world revolved from night to day,
A voice, a chime, a chant sublime,
Of peace on earth, good will to men!

HENRY WADSWORTH LONGFELLOW.

## A CHRISTMAS PRAYER

We open here our treasures and our gifts;
And some of it is gold,
And some is frankincense,
And some is myrrh;
For some has come from plenty,
Some from joy,

And some from deepest sorrow of the soul.
But Thou, O God, dost know the gift is love,
Our pledge of peace, our promise of good will.
Accept the gift and all the life we bring.

HERBERT H. HINES.

## CHRISTMAS PRAYER

Let Christmas not become a thing
Merely of merchants' trafficking,

Of tinsel, bell and holly wreath
And surface pleasure, but beneath

The childish glamor let us find
Nourishment for soul and mind.

Let us follow kinder ways
Through our teeming human maze

And help the age of peace to come
From a dreamer's martyrdom.

MADELINE MORSE.

## CHRISTMAS TODAY

The grinding machinery of a throbbing world stands
still;
The city streets are strangely quiet;
A brooding hush enfolds the snow-draped hill;
There's a rustle of wings.

Fresh-fanned to life are sacred fires
And like holy incense tender thoughts arise.
The mystic breath of a spirit world
Revives within hearts, long fast locked,
Kindly musings and kindlier purpose.
Hands are outstretched and laden
With gold, incense and myrrh.
A world, heart-hungry and expectant,
Crowds eagerly the manger door.

E. G. REITH.

## EARTH LISTENS

At last our dull Earth listens:
Peace! Good will!
The Star of Bethlehem glistens
Nearer, nearer still.

Holy luster christens
War-torn heath and hill.
At last, at last Earth listens:
Peace! Good will!

KATHARINE LEE BATES.

## IN BETHLEHEM, TODAY

His light still shines in Bethlehem Town
Where long-limbed camels stately stalk
And matrons virtuously walk
In spotless headdress flowing down
About their ample-skirted gown.

## CHRISTMAS

His light still shines in children's eyes
That nightly feast on starry skies
    And intimately know the sheep
    That shepherds on their hillside keep
    On nights too heavenly for sleep.

His light still shines above the lamps
In shrines where creeds make hostile camps;
    For not in incense-stifled air
    His Presence breathes, but yonder where
    The people walk in Bethlehem square.

MADELEINE SWEENY MILLER.

## EPIPHANY

*In the path of the silver Star,*
*Three kings rode,*
*Rode to quiet Bethlehem*
*Where God that night abode.*

One brought him gleaming gold, a gift from a king to a
    King,
And he bent his haughty head in humble worshipping
Before the living gold that haloed the baby thing.

One brought frankincense, and sweet grew the dim low
    place—
But a rarer fragrance came, like the blessing of infinite
    grace,
From the little Rose of God, as he lay in His mother's
    embrace.

And the third gave myrrh to Him—symbol of lordly doom—
But, dark behind mother and Child, weft on no mortal loom,
Deeper than earthly night, sad shadows bordered the room.

*Silent the kings rode home,*
*Theirs the greater gain—*
*The gifts the Child gave them—*
*His love and life and pain.*

KATHERINE BURTON.

## THE THREE MAGI

They lost the Star one night. (Why do men lose
The Star? Sometimes because they gaze too hard.)
The two White Kings called back Chaldean lore,
Traced on the ground great circles with a staff,
Added, subtracted, stroked their troubled chins,
In vain. The Star, their kindly guide, had fled.
And these learned men, who knew their ignorance,
Seeing no issue, pitched their tents and wept.
But the Black King, whom these looked down upon,
Shook off his grief and said, "Because I thirst,
I must not fail to give the camels drink."

And while he held a vessel for the beasts
He saw the water catch a bit of sky,
And in its humble circle danced the Star.

ROY TEMPLE HOUSE.

## CHRISTMAS CAROL

The earth has grown old with its burden of care,
  But at Christmas it always is young.
The heart of the jewel burns lustrous and fair,
And its soul full of music breaks forth on the air,
  When the song of the angels is sung.

It is coming, old earth, it is coming tonight!
  On the snowflakes that covered thy sod
The feet of the Christ-child fall gentle and white
And the voice of the Christ-child tells out
  That mankind are the children of God.

On the sad and the lonely, the wretched and poor,
  The voice of the Christ-child shall fall;
And to every blind wanderer open the door
Of a hope that he dared not to dream of before,
  With a sunshine of welcome for all.

The feet of the humblest may walk in the field
  Where the feet of the holiest have trod,
This, this is the marvel to mortals revealed
When the silvery trumpets of Christmas have pealed,
  That mankind are the children of God.

PHILLIPS BROOKS.

## A CHRISTMAS CAROL

There's a song in the air!
There's a star in the sky!
There's a mother's deep prayer
And a baby's low cry!
And the star rains its fire while the Beautiful sing,
For the manger of Bethlehem cradles a King.

There's a tumult of joy
O'er the wonderful birth,
For the virgin's sweet boy
Is the Lord of the earth,
Ay! the star rains its fire and the Beautiful sing,
For the manger of Bethlehem cradles a King.

In the light of that star
Lie the ages impearled;
And the song from afar
Has swept over the world.
Every hearth is aflame and the Beautiful sing
In the homes of the nations that Jesus is King.

We rejoice in the light,
And we echo the song
That comes down through the night
From the heavenly throng.
Ay! we shout to the lovely evangel they bring,
And we greet in his cradle our Savior and King!

JOSIAH GILBERT HOLLAND.

## NOEL! NOEL!

Oh Christmas, that your Gift of Gifts might be
Amongst us yet! as once in Galilee—
Telling of lilies, and of birds overhead—
Of little children and our daily bread—
To us, His humble fisher-folk! make plain
The shining wonder of Himself again,
That we may touch the seamless garment's rim
And be made whole, through the dear grace of Him!
Across the centuries that seem so far—
How close the Christ Child comes! how near the Star!

LAURA SIMMONS.

## NOT KINGS

Hostlers and shepherds hailed His birth,
And cattle from their stall;
But also from the rim of earth
There came some few to fall

Upon their knees beside His bed
Of camel-cloths and hay
And glimpse the glory of His head,
Not found in night or day.

They were not kings, these pilgrims three
Who from the eastward came;
Their worn cloaks showed their poverty,
Their feet were torn and lame.

Oh yes, I know the lying tale
Which monarchs later told,
How each one rode upon a bale
Of spices, silk and gold.

But never kings, again I say,
Would cross the desert wild
Westward from Ind or from Cathay
To greet this Poor Man's Child.

Only one king had thought of Him.
He wrenched his crimson beard
And gnawed his goblet's golden rim.
From cunning eye-slits peered

About the room, as if in fear;
Gulped down the wine he'd poured,
And whispered fiercely in the ear
Of one who held a sword.

KENNETH W. PORTER.

## THE HOLY THORN

Long centuries past by lonely barrows grew
The faery hawthorn boughs of haunted green,
Beneath whose shade the Danaan gods unseen
Awoke slain heroes dark with battle-dew;
Their gilded shields of apple-wood and yew
In time's deep tumulus have lost their sheen,
Yet where these blossom-laden branches lean
The faith of vanished ages blooms anew.

One ancient miracle enduring still,
Though earth's old magic seems a myth outworn,
Has hallowed Avalon's enchanted hill;
For when men hymn the Son of God reborn,
Although December woods are bare and chill,
At wintry Christ-tide flowers the Holy Thorn.

THOMAS S. JONES, JR.

## THE LORD OF THE WORLD

Come sail with me o'er the golden sea
To the land where the rainbow ends,
Where the rainbow ends,
And the great earth bends
To the weight of the starry sky,
Where the tempests die with a last fierce cry,
And never a wind is wild.
There's a Mother mild, with a little Child
Like a star set on her knee,
Then bow you down, give Him the crown
'Tis the Lord of the world you see.

G. A. STUDDERT-KENNEDY.

## A CHRISTMAS PRAYER

"The star stood over where the young child was—"
Only a star was high enough to mark
Thy cradle, O Thou Holy One of earth!
Was bright enough to point men through the dark
Since that glad night of old that saw Thy birth!

For stars belong to the unbounded skies;
Stars are not found beneath the roofs of creed,
Nor reached by straining spires of steel and stone:
Alike they shine to serve a whole world's need,
That none dare cry, "The stars are mine alone!"

O Star beyond all stars, the darkness still
Is slow to comprehend! O Light of men,
The glare of earth has kept us blind so long!
Forgive us as we lift our eyes again,
And make us brave to live the angels' song!

MOLLY ANDERSON HALEY.

# ACKNOWLEDGMENTS

Acknowledgment is here made of the generous cooperation of both contributing poets and publishers in the bringing together of this anthology.

The compiler has made every effort to trace the ownership of all poems. To the best of his knowledge he has secured necessary permission from authors or their authorized agents. Should there prove to be any question regarding the use of any poem, the compiler herewith expresses regret for any such unconscious error. He will be pleased, upon notification of any oversight on his part, to make proper acknowledgment in future editions of the book.

Acknowledgments to Publishers: Doubleday, Doran & Co., poems of Studdert Kennedy, Oxenham, Kipling and Burr. Charles Scribner's Sons, poems by Henry van Dyke. Macmillan Co., poems by Tennyson. Houghton Mifflin & Co., poems by Longfellow, Lowell, Holmes, Whittier, Emerson, and Thompson. Little, Brown & Co., poems by Susan Coolidge. Fleming H. Revell Co., poem by W. J. Dawson. Powell & White, poem by Clara C. Leland. Meigs Publishing Co., poem by C. D. Meigs. T. Y. Crowell Co., poems by Katharine L. Bates. The Century Co., poem by James Oppenheim, from his volume, "War and Laughter"; poem by S. Weir Mitchell, from his "Complete Poems." G. P. Putnam's Sons, poem by Lyman W. Allen. W. B. Conkey Co., poem by Ella Wheeler Wilcox, from her volume, "Poems of Power." The Beacon Press, the poem "Our Country" by F. L. Hosmer, from his volume "The Thought of God," copyright by The Beacon Press, Inc., used with permission. Carrollton Publishing Co., poem by Denis A. McCarthy, from his volume

## ACKNOWLEDGMENTS

"The Harp of Life." Henry Holt & Co., poem by Carl Sandburg, from his volume, "Chicago Poems." E. P. Dutton & Co., "Christmas Carol" by Phillips Brooks, used by special permission. Reilly & Lee, poem by W. D. Nesbit, used by special permission from his volume, "Paths from Long Age," copyrighted 1926. Harr Wagner Publishing Co., poem by Joaquin Miller, from his volume, "Favorite Poems." Methodist Book Concern, poems by J. T. McFarland from his volume "Poems," and Poems by Frances C. Hamlet.

Acknowledgments to Periodicals: The Christian Advocate, poems by Madeleine S. Miller, E. G. Reith, R. S. Cushman and L. S. Uphoff. The Presbyterian Advance, poem by Janie Alford. The Classmate, poem by Clinton Scollard ("The Way to Bethlehem," and by T. C. Clark ("Song of Christian Workingmen"). Saturday Review of Literature, poem by K. W. Porter ("Not Kings"). The Churchman, poems by Maud F. Jackson, Alta B. Dunn, Molly A. Haley and Kenneth W. Porter ("A Christmas Prayer"). The Living Church, poems by Katherine Burton, Thomas S. Jones, Jr., and George Klingle ("The Wounded Christ-Heart"). The Watchman-Examiner, poems by G. H. Osborne and George Klingle ("Palm Sunday Hymn"). The Atlanta Constitution, poem by F. L. Stanton. Unity, poems by E. K. Biddle, Clifford Gessler, Madeleine Morse and Raymond Kresensky ("The End of the World"). The Baptist, poem by Robert Whitaker. The Christian Century, poems by Ethel R. Fuller, Raymond Kresensky, Edward Shillito, E. Merrill Root, C. G. Blanden, H. H. Hines, T. C. Clark, Helen M. Salisbury and Laura Simmons.

Special acknowledgment is made to Edwin Markham for permission to reprint four poems from his "Collected Poems." To Elias Liebermann for the use of his "I Am an American," on which he holds copyright. Also to many other poets who granted personal permission to include selections from their work in this anthology.

THE COMPILER